To Ron, Xmas 2003. from Mary
x x x x

D1631843

German Naval
Code Breakers

German Naval
Code Breakers

Jak P. Mallmann Showell

Ian Allan
PUBLISHING

First published 2003

ISBN 0 7110 2888 5

All rights reserved. No part of this book may be reproduced or transmitted in any form or by any means, electronic or mechanical, including photocopying, recording or by any information storage and retrieval system, without permission from the Publisher in writing.

© Jak P. Mallmann Showell 2003

The right of Jak P. Mallmann Showell to be identified as the author of this work has been asserted by him in accordance with the Copyright, Designs and Patents Act 1988.

Published by Ian Allan Publishing

an imprint of Ian Allan Publishing Ltd, Hersham, Surrey KT12 4RG.
Printed by Ian Allan Printing Ltd, Hersham, Surrey KT12 4RG.

Code: 0304/A3

Picture Credits
Photographs, unless credited otherwise, are reproduced from the author's collection or courtesy of the U-Boot Archiv, 27478 Cuxhaven-Altenbruch (Germany).

Contents

Introduction & Acknowledgements

The history of the German Naval Radio Monitoring Service or Funkbeobachtungsdienst, better known as the B-Dienst, is still clouded in deep mystery. Surprisingly, many naval histories scarcely mention it and there appear to be no specialists' books in English on this fascinating subject. The wartime leader of the B-Dienst, Kapitän-zur-See (KptzS) Heinz Bonatz, produced two publications in German, but the first of these has vanished into obscurity and is exceedingly difficult to find these days. The other, his main work, contains a vast quantity of abbreviations, some of them without explanations, which make it hard to understand. Yet, despite this, it does provide an intriguing insight into this obscure subject.

The lack of knowledge of the German Radio Monitoring Service is not confined to historians, but also extended into wartime activities. Heinz Bonatz was captured by British forces at the end of the war and taken to the prisoner-of-war-cum-concentration camp at Neuengamme (Hamburg), but never interrogated about his amazing interception, decoding and intelligence activities. Now, it seems as if these important aspects of naval history have slipped almost into total oblivion. I hope that this book will spur people on to contribute any information they may still have. The U-Boot-Archiv (D-27478 Cuxhaven-Altenbruch, Germany) would be delighted to hear from anyone harbouring material about this now almost forgotten aspect of German naval history.

This book contains a pot-pourri of material to illustrate some of the achievements of the Radio Monitoring Service, rather than another chronological history of the war at sea. I hope that the views expressed in the following pages reflect the thoughts of the people who worked there at the time, and I have made a considerable effort not to amend these in accordance with postwar attitudes.

I should like to thank Horst Bredow of the U-Boot-Archiv for allowing me to search through the dark recesses of the Archiv for evidence of Radio Monitoring activities and I am grateful to the Archiv for contributing photographs. I am also grateful to Margaret Bidmead of the Royal Navy Submarine Museum for her support. I have used notes compiled during the last 20 years with the help of people who were involved with naval radio and radar, namely Wolfgang Hirschfeld, KptzS aD (ausser Dienst - retired) Otto Köhler, Dr Joachim Kindler, KptzS aD 'Ajax' Bleichrodt, Professor Heinfried Ahl and Karl Wahnig. In addition to these, I should like to thank the many people who have kindly left so many interesting reminiscences in the U-Boot-Archiv for future historians to uncover. Stephen Hunt must be thanked for allowing me to photograph the remains of the radar station near Dungeness and for explaining the meaning of the relics on his land. I would also like to thank Thomas Zingsheim for contributing some photographs, and Bernhard Schlummer for providing information.

Above: This huge concrete sound mirror on The Roughs in Hythe (Kent) is one of several similar relics which remind us of how times have changed. It was built at the same time as the B-Dienst was re-establishing itself as a vital part of the German Navy, shortly after World War 1, but the detector had hardly been finished when radar was perfected to make a sound collection system obsolete. Originally it had a funnel in the centre of the cup to transfer sounds down a pipe to an operator sitting in a tiny underground control room. Yet, despite modern technology, this particular sound mirror was wired with microphones during World War 2 as a backup in case radar masts were put out of action.

Chapter 1
The Radio Monitoring Service

The peace terms dictated by the Allies at the end of World War 1 demanded that the majority of Germany's weapons and military-industrial plant be handed over to the victors, destroyed or, at least, drastically reduced in size. On top of this, Germany had to disclose its military, technological and national secrets, and all this took place while the country slumped into uncontrollable depression. A high proportion of the breadwinners were out of work and there was a drastic shortage of food and fuel for heating homes during exceptionally cold winters. This, together with expensive war reparations, led to the collapse of the monetary system and public services, reducing the nation to a pitiful state of destitution. There was also talk of disbanding the Navy and passing the few remaining, antiquated ships over to army control, but despite several minor rebellions, mutinies and localised uprisings, the remains of the once proud Imperial Navy maintained a firm grip on its autonomy, to emerge as a small, insignificant force, which was just about capable of maintaining law and order in its immediate coastal waters.

The Kaiser's highly successful Radio Monitoring Service had been so secret that many administrators responsible for the shrinking of the military were not even aware of its existence, but they knew full well the majority of naval radio stations had to be scrapped. Therefore, it was easy to demob everything connected with the subject. Only the commanding officer, Kapitänleutnant (Kptlt) Braune was spared, but he was called to Berlin to write an account of what his departments had accomplished during the war, rather than to build upon the solid foundations already laid down. His rank of Kapitänleutnant or lieutenant-commander indicates that this important aspect of naval warfare had not been terribly high on the list of priorities. The exact details of his achievements seem to have vanished into obscurity, together with all copies of his official history. Yet he had hardly started his mammoth undertaking when a number of influential sea-going officers noticed how officialdom had disbanded one of their most useful aids. Consequently, less than a year after the end of the war, Braune was asked to re-establish naval radio monitoring and decoding facilities and by May 1919 each of these had a departmental head from the Civil Service plus a staff of about half a dozen or so. The reason for not employing naval officers was because the Navy had been shrunk to such a small size that there were hardly enough men to crew the few remaining ships. Even Braune, a naval officer and the father of this new outfit, did not last long

with his new baby. He was discharged before the end of the year so that the Navy would fit into the requirements demanded by the victorious Allies.

From then on, the Radio Monitoring Service stumbled on in splendid isolation, without too much interruption from the massive bureaucratic system which steered the German military. The majority of naval officers were totally unaware these departments existed and the few employees who worked there were content to establish the bare bones, such as efficient radio sets, for gaining a foothold in what was becoming an increasingly complicated subject. Not only was the technology improving, but secret codes were becoming more and more difficult to unravel. This slow but steady progress continued for 10 years until October 1929, when someone struck upon the idea of replacing the civilian heads of what were then the Radio Reconnaissance Unit and the Deciphering Department with naval officers. Although this sounds like a step in the right direction, the decision was taken as a cost-saving venture to prevent the Treasury from paying the salaries of two high-grade civil servants. At the same time, the two departments were moved to Kiel because staff there were not eligible for the salary supplement for working in the state capital, Berlin. For security reasons, neither of these departments had their correct names on their doors and no one seemed concerned about these vital tools being shunted into what was then a provincial backwater, isolated from the decision makers in the Supreme Naval Command. Although there were technically two different divisions, they had actually grown into three departments, known simply as AIII, which was divided into A3a for Intelligence Communication, for transmission of news; A3b for Radio Reconnaissance, including the development of the Navy's own cipher system; and Group FM (*Fremde Marinen*), dealing with foreign navies.

Much of the work was devoted to the creation of new German ciphers, code books and so forth, rather than listening for and decoding foreign signals, and it was the Radio Reconnaissance branch, A3b, which first worked with the now famous Enigma machine and studied how to make its workings more secure, adding the so-called plug board to the design. This work occupied the code breakers until the mid-1930s when a standard naval version of the machine was finally introduced. In the same years the Army's code-breaking activities began to be directed largely against Poland, which had been newly created from territory which before World War 1 had belonged to Germany, Austria and Russia. However,

Above: Wind-up record players have become collectors' items and are now used to add nostalgia for re-enactment groups, but before the war they were the only way people could enjoy listening to recorded music in their own homes. Even then, such record players were terribly expensive and the majority of workers could not afford to buy them. The picture of Adolf Hitler in the background suggests this photograph dates from after 1935. He came to power in 1933, but photographs of him did not appear in naval quarters until a couple of years later.

since East Prussia was divided from the rest of Germany by the so-called Polish Corridor, the Navy was not too keen on establishing bases in the far eastern Baltic. The admirals felt that supplying such strongholds in times of conflict could turn into a logistical nightmare. However, the government was keen on boosting the flagging economy in the east and encouraged a variety of shipping activities by providing more than generous grants for all sorts of industrial development in those areas.

In 1935, when Hitler repudiated the Treaty — or 'Dictate', as he called it — of Versailles, created new defence laws, and reintroduced conscription, the staff of the Radio Monitoring Service consisted of about 20 men divided between the three departments already mentioned. Plans were made to bring them back to Berlin and, at the same time, enlarge the staff to about 120–130. However, this projected strength had not even been reached by the time World War 2 started in September 1939. A fourth department was added in 1935 for the purpose of collecting information from the foreign press, other similar public sources and collating news trickling in from naval attachés around the globe. Although this should have led to an enlargement of the service generally, it resulted instead in a hive of empire building, with each group trying to outdo the other,

rather than devising some means of co-operation. Incidentally, in those days Germany had naval attachés in Ankara, Brussels, Buenos Aires, Copenhagen, The Hague, Helsinki, Lisbon, London, Madrid, Moscow, Oslo, Paris, Rome, Stockholm, Tokyo, Washington and Zagreb (Yugoslavia).

Bringing naval personnel back into the Radio Monitoring Service resulted in some rather interesting discoveries and made it clear how high-grade civil servants struggled unnecessarily with naval terminology. People were devoting considerable resources to decoding what were straightforward naval terms, thinking that seamen's slang was a form of secret code. In view of this, it was decided that future staff should be drawn from naval personnel with excellent linguistic abilities, rather than civilians. The problem with this decision was that it became exceedingly difficult to find the right type of people and such exacting work could not be left to semi-enthusiastic sailors with a powerful urge to get away from the rigours of life aboard warships. It quickly became evident that one not only needed people with a special type of brain, but it was also necessary to invest considerable time in training them. These thoughts were simmering in the great bureaucratic cauldron when the Spanish Civil War brought the entire concept of radio

Above: The old Elbe Tunnel in Hamburg at the end of the late afternoon shift change. The landing stages were not built for the benefit of tourists but to provide easy access to a mass of small ferries taking workers into the port. The clock tower in the distance, which is difficult to make out against the background clutter, also served as an information source by displaying the state of the tide for passing ships.

monitoring into new and larger significance. Suddenly the ability to read other nation's codes was transferred from an idle, academic exercise to a terrific advantage. Activities in Spanish waters made the naval hierarchy realise that the planned strength of the Radio Monitoring Service, mentioned above, had never been attained and, at the same time, the new developments in Spain gave the small departments the muscle they needed to mark their significance on the map. However, secrecy demanded they still refrained from pinning their true identification on their doors.

Although still relatively small in size and limited in performance, considerable progress had been made since 1919, when much of the radio hardware was thrown on the scrap heap. This was a period when radio was still very much in its infancy and the many houses in country districts did not even have electricity. The absence of such basic resources, which are taken so much for granted today, meant the majority of new radio stations had to be built with their own services such as electricity generators. The absence of a cable network added considerable problems to the setting up of the radio direction finders, and the laying of direct telephone cables over vast distances was needed to make this process work.

Two chains of coastal radio stations were developed by the early 1930s: one for the North Sea and the other for the Baltic. The southernmost location in the west was situated on the Friesian island of Borkum, close to the Dutch border, while the other end of the chain terminated at List on the Island of Sylt, the northernmost village (or rather cluster of houses) in Germany. In between, was a third outpost on the old airship base at Nordholz near Cuxhaven and these three had their main control centre at Wilhelmshaven, Germany's biggest North Sea naval base. These were all equipped with receivers, transmitters and radio direction finders. Even the smallest outposts were capable of eavesdropping on all sorts of radio transmissions and, at the same time, determining accurately the direction the signals were coming from. Specially laid direct telephone cables connected all four, making it unnecessary even to dial a number in order to communicate over the secure land lines, without interfering with any radio signals.

The Baltic radio chain started at Falshöft, then a tiny coastal community of a few houses near Flensburg, close to the Danish border. Before the war, it was so isolated that there was not even a decently surfaced road, making it quite a long trek over cobblestones and pot-holed lanes to get there. The next link of this coastal chain was on Cape Arkona, so remote that one is likely to overlook

Above: Long-distance international travel has changed beyond recognition. In the days when the B-Dienst was being established hardly anyone, other than officials or very rich film stars, travelled by air. Even then, aircraft did not fly far and they could only take off when the weather permitted. Anyone going further afield had to travel by ship. This shows a luxurious liner at the Überseebrücke (Overseas Pier) in Hamburg before the war. The newly built underground railway had to go high up on pedestal supports by the side of the river because exceptionally high tides usually flooded the roads. The massive metal framework in the background shows the gantry type of cranes at the Stülkenwerft shipyard and the cranes towards the right belong to the famous ship building company Blohm und Voss.

it on non-German atlases. It is in fact the north-eastern tip of Rügen, Germany's largest island. There was another fairly isolated radio base at Stolpmünde (now Ustka), by the western coastal edge of the new Polish Corridor, some 120 kilometres west of Danzig (now Gdansk). In addition to this, there were bigger facilities at Pillau (Baltysk), the easternmost location; at the naval base in Swinemünde (Swmoujscie), and at the main naval base in Kiel. There was also a backup at Neumünster, roughly halfway between Kiel and Hamburg. These two base lines were ideal for triangulation within the Baltic and North Sea, but did not provide sufficient length for covering more distant waters. Therefore, another radio station was established near Soest, between Dortmund and Bielefeld, to help lengthen the base line for the direction finders and this was later supplemented by more bases further south.

Once two or more radio stations obtained bearings on a radio transmission, it was a simple case of some applied geometry to calculate the position of the sender. A set of protractors fitted onto a specially built plotting table with chart was used to obtain a quick result. These instruments appear to have vanished into obscurity, but a few years ago there was a British example in the Royal Artillery Museum in Woolwich (London). Although apparently not so accurate as detailed calculations, these tables did provide an instant position, good enough to help a lost ship or aircraft out of difficulties. English Heritage has also re-created such a plotting table in the operations centre of the catacombs under Dover Castle. This consists of a large chart with tape measures, marked in miles, attached to the various direction finder stations. They were pulled to the correct angles and thus provided an instant position of the source. The Germans are known to have used something similar. Sadly the author was not allowed to photograph the reconstruction in Dover to show what it looked like. It had been assembled only a short time before his visit and the flash from the camera would have damaged the colour of the paint used in re-creating this wartime scene.

Today, with wireless communications having become so commonplace, it is easy to forget that these early developments were taking place during a pioneering period of technology, when much of the equipment was heavy, cumbersome and fragile, and messages were often muffled by a multitude of background noises. However, progress was swift and by the time World War 2 ended, equipment had been reduced in size so that a man could carry a portable radio transmitter together with the battery needed to operate it.

Despite this rapid improvement, many ships continued plying their trade along the European coastal routes without radio until well after World War 2 and visual communication continued to play a vital role. The radio station aboard the Borkumriff (Borkum Sandbank) Lightship, for example, was used as a reporting base. Ships wishing their position to be passed on would hoist appropriate flags. The sighting was then reported by radio to the old Borkum lighthouse and from there sent by land line to Emden and on to shipping authorities in the main ports. At this time radios were not yet powerful enough to reach Emden, or any of the other ports direct, and the land-line connection was vital.

The difficulties of making this technology work can, perhaps, be illustrated by the southernmost naval radio station, which was set up during the 1920s on top of a hill near Villingen in the Black Forest. The small Reichsmarine had run out of its allocation of resources as permitted by the Treaty of Versailles and therefore disguised this location as an army unit, but its main purpose was to provide a broader base for naval triangulation bearings. A variety of reasons prevented clear reception, despite the aerials being high up on a hill, and there was nothing technicians could do to improve matters. None of the modifications worked, leaving enough natural inference to make it difficult or even impossible to obtain accurate bearings. This resulted in the station being dismantled after a year and moved to a site near Landsberg on the River Lech. After World War 2 this area became a major NATO radio centre with a massive circular aerial, looking something like Stonehenge, but made from iron girders instead of stones. The Spanish Civil War and general progress with radio reception resulted in another station being built later at Langenargen on Lake Constance, about halfway between Friedrichshafen and Lindau. Later another one was added at Neusiedl-am-See in Austria. It is rather odd, but the building of the main station near Berlin, close to the Supreme Naval Command, was planned but never started.

As things turned out, the accuracy of these stations' performance was responsible for diverting them from their main objective of monitoring foreign radio broadcasts. The German Navy discovered it was easy for the direction finders to get extremely accurate bearings on transmitters at sea and, therefore, by installing similar gear on ships, it was also possible to get directions from ships to beacons by these stations. This put the difficulty of navigating through the North Sea shallows into a totally new light and the Navy started using the facilities

for finding its way during overcast periods, when it was impossible to obtain accurate fixes on the sun or stars.

As with many bureaucratic organisations, as early as the 1920s there were administrators sitting in comfortable offices thinking about how they could check up on men stationed in these isolated outposts. After all, the Navy needed a system to keep them at work, rather than have them sloping off to go bird watching, hunting or fishing. The solution was simple. The radio operators were told to compile log books with their observations and these were then compared with those from other stations. This mass of paperwork became an administrators' paradise and the cracking of foreign codes was relegated into second place. In any case, the exact meaning of these messages was not high on the list priorities and it was more a case of finding out how other countries were using radio. This was indeed one of the early weak links. Technological development was rapid, so keeping a grip on this progress became a vital task for the Radio Monitoring Service. To explore this further, monitoring facilities were set up aboard warships going on foreign tours, to keep a watch along far-off shores. A few spy ships, disguised as fishing boats, also sailed through international waters of the North Sea close to Britain, but these were only occasional, temporary expeditions and the German Radio Monitoring Service did not employ spy ships on a permanent basis. Records of military receivers being fitted to merchant ships for the purpose of exploring foreign radio transmissions have not been found.

During the late 1920s, the radio monitoring stations were sufficiently well developed for them to settle into their peacetime roles of helping commercial shipping. Nordholz near Cuxhaven, for example, became a radio direction finding station for international traffic in the North Sea. Even on a mundane, daily basis radio provided great advantages. The arrival time of ships had always been difficult to forecast and radio made the administration of ports much easier. The other major innovation of the time, which has already been mentioned, was connecting these outlying coastal bases by telephone and telex land lines to their immediate control centres and also to the Supreme Naval Command in Berlin. Telex was a forerunner of the modern e-mail system. It used telephone cables to send written text from one typewriter-like machine to another. During the early 1930s most of these isolated coastal stations submitted on average some 2,500 intercepted messages each month to a central office in Berlin. So the system was quite busy and offices with these percussion machines were exceedingly noisy.

In addition to their peacetime roles, the coastal radio stations, their control centres in the major towns and the main hub in Berlin were all included in the emergency military mobilisation plans as follows:

1. Kiel, Wilhelmshaven, Neumünster and Swinemünde were assigned to intercept and record British radio signals.
2. Langenargen on Lake Constance and Soest dealt with the French and Italians.
3. Neusiedl-am-See (Austria) and Pillau dealt with the Russians.
4. Pillau and Swinemünde dealt with the Poles.

By the time Hitler came to power, it was obvious that setting up the hardware for these stations, which had been built in the 1920s, was considerably easier than getting the right people to operate it, and finding the right type of person for breaking the codes was even harder. Britain got over this hurdle with a crossword competition in the *Daily Telegraph* newspaper. Many of those who sent in the correct answers were invited to have a go at another, similar, competition where time was of the essence. The people who managed this successfully were then invited for an interview to see whether they might be suitable for such exacting tasks as breaking codes. In Germany the bureaucracy took the view that people with these special qualities were already somewhere in the armed forces and it was only a matter of pushing them into the right post. This paid meagre dividends, producing only a small number of suitable people, and also leaving vast gaps in the system. The problem of code breakers not being required to be jacks-of-all-trades but near experts in every subject was not yet realised. They needed a wide general knowledge and also had to be capable of spotting the unusual. They had to draw inferences from the most innocuous pieces of information. It wasn't so much a case of keeping an occasional eye on a potential enemy's objectives, but getting to know the opposition so well as almost to become part of it.

Of course, there were a number of officers in the German Navy with such qualities, but enticing them into the code-breaking service was not easy. After all, the majority joined to go to sea, not to sit in stuffy offices on land. What's more, getting access to the best men in the Navy was no simple matter. The high-profile posts always tended to have priority over 'secret' occupations such as code breaking. The other snag was that the requirements for code breakers conflicted considerably with the Navy's policy of allowing the majority of officers to remain in a job for only one year. October was the month when positions were shuffled around and men looked for new pastures. This may be ideal for people manning ships at sea, but it took the best part of a year to acquaint code breakers with their jobs. This problem of getting the right people remained throughout the reign of the Third Reich and from 1935 onwards the Radio Monitoring Service always had to rely on a core of inexperienced newcomers who required considerable training before they could tackle the tasks expected of them.

The B-Dienst was not the only organisation involved with the deciphering of foreign radio codes. Both the German Army and Foreign Office devoted equal or greater resources to similar objectives. There was some co-operation in the field of cracking codes, but generally rivalry and internal suspicion prevented the sharing of too many secrets. This state of affairs became even worse after 1935 when the Luftwaffe was founded and also embarked on code-breaking activities. The Foreign Office in particular was more concerned with keeping the military well clear of diplomatic ciphers, than with encouraging cross-fertilisation of ideas and efforts. The barriers between these departments became wider as World War 2 progressed, partly because the Supreme Naval Command was not satisfied with the standards of security being adopted by the Army and Air Force. The low standards were partly due to sloppy procedures, but also to different specifications demanded by the different services. For example, both the Army and Air Force were keen to have simple, small and highly portable coding machines which needed to maintain their secrecy for only a relatively short period of time. The Navy, on the other hand, moved much more slowly and therefore modified the basic Enigma machine with a complicated plug board to add a vast amount of variations to the theme. This line of thought also extended to the deciphering process, where the Navy was quite happy to work much longer in order to decode messages.

While the Enigma machines were being developed, the Navy had already discovered that considerable information could be extracted from radio signals, even when it was impossible to decipher their meanings. It was often possible to work out exactly where the enemy was likely to go, merely by plotting radio messages over a period of time. In view of this, the Navy objected most strongly to both Army and Luftwaffe practices of sending virtually all their communications by radio, even if the code was considered to be unbreakable. The Navy adopted the principle of shutting down ship-based radio rooms as soon as secure land lines became available in port. To facilitate this the Navy ran cables out to the larger buoys in the main harbours, making it possible for ships' commanders to talk directly to the higher officers ashore.

In addition to co-operation between various interest spheres within Germany, the Radio Monitoring Service also worked with foreign establishments. This came about for two reasons: because high-ranking naval officers were keen on exchanging information, or because the government suggested a close involvement. Of course, such co-operation was possible only with 'friendly' states which shared a potential common enemy. The countries with which the sharing of code-breaking ideas was possible were Bulgaria, Finland, Hungary, Italy, Portugal, Spain, Sweden and Turkey.

Above: Tape recorders appeared during the war and transformed radio monitoring. They made it possible for messages to be recorded and therefore took a great weight off operators, who up to that period of time had no way of getting a repeat of anything they had heard. This equipment was installed inside *U552* during the war. Yet, although such equipment was available, it still remained extremely expensive.

Above and opposite: The old signal tower by the Blücher Pier in Kiel. Although looking like a medieval lighthouse, it was built for naval communications and remained in use until World War 2, when another signal tower was established further out towards the open Baltic. Approaching ships had to make visual contact before entering the narrows of the vast inlet leading to the naval base. There was a mast for hoisting flags and a platform for semaphore, although Morse code became an increasingly popular way of sending and receiving messages. Warships coming into a naval base usually telephoned from their last port of call to announce their estimated time of arrival and were told by visual means where to berth after they had been sighted. In some places the signal stations doubled up as pilot bases and along the North Sea coast they also provided visual information about the state of the tide. Surfaced U-boats were just as difficult to spot from land stations as they were from ships at sea and the bolder commanders used the opportunity of creeping up unseen on the observers, to surprise them with rude flashes from their signal lamp. A note on the back of the next photograph indicates it shows the commissioning of U50 by Max-Hermann Bauer on 12 December 1939.

Today it is exceedingly difficult to trace the story of such co-operation. Much of the work was already under way at around the time Hitler came to power, but later a number of the countries dropped out of the initiative.

Prewar progress with international co-operation was more than satisfactory and the stringent demands laid down by the Radio Monitoring Service were often attained. Even small countries with limited resources, such as Finland, were known to have gained a deep insight into complicated foreign ciphers, and this spurred German analysts on with powerful incentives to beat such performances.

Although this meticulous work was a continuous, ongoing process, the real tests came during the naval manoeuvres of Germany's potential enemies, when foreign navies were rehearsing their secret plans for future conflict. This was an occasion when it definitely was not good enough for radio intercept operators to supply the occasional insight into what was going on, and considerable effort had to be made to keep tabs on individual transmitting stations, to record every one of their many broadcasts. This task alone presented numerous difficulties, making it quite an achievement to have intercepted so many messages.

Through keeping tabs on manoeuvres, the Supreme Naval Command got to know valuable information about the readiness of foreign fleets, their ship movements, their main concerns and the tactics they were likely to employ. For example, it quickly became obvious that Britain was still developing the convoy system which it had employed during World War 1. Radio intercepts showed the Royal Navy was practising defending convoys as well as finding good ways of attacking them. It also became evident that Britain was putting considerable emphasis on its secret underwater detecting device for finding submerged submarines.

All in all, even before World War 2 began, the Kriegsmarine's B-Dienst was already achieving a great deal. Germany was right at the cutting edge of this new field.

Above and left:
The high, red sandstone cliffs of Heligoland with their contrasting yellow sand had this military observation tower built on top to increase the field of view for lookouts. The small number of tiny windows, with iron shutters, suggest this was built to protect observers in times of attack rather than as a civilian lighthouse. The Treaty of Versailles dictated that all such military installations on Heligoland had to be removed after World War 1, which would suggest this imposing structure was built sometime after 1935.

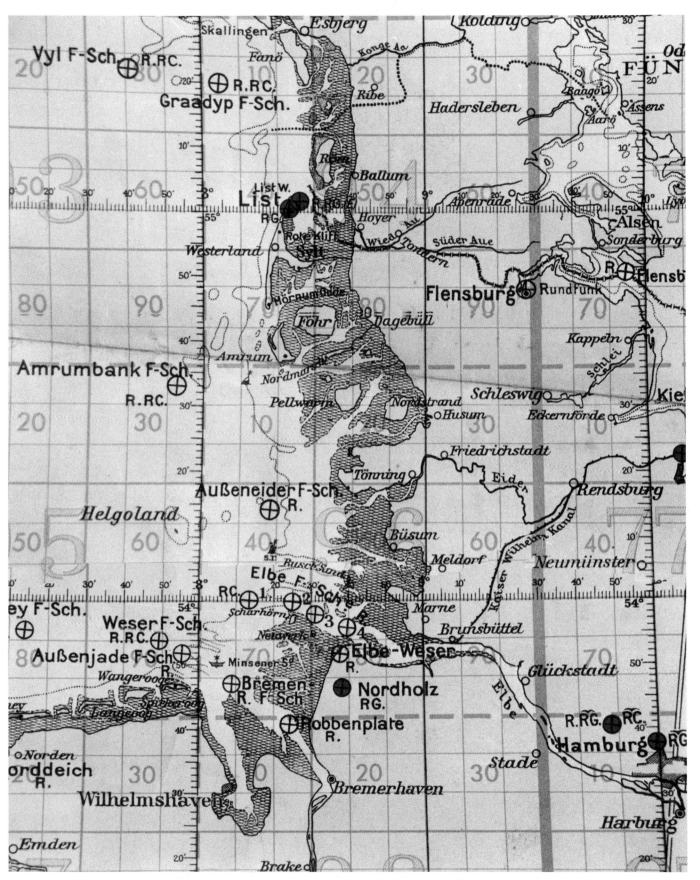

Above: The German coast shown on a wartime radio location map of the North Sea, marking the major radio transmitters.

Above:
Looking across the harbour basin at Cuxhaven from the old passenger terminal towards Alte Liebe, with the early lighthouse on the left and two more modern shipping control towers towards the right. The old lighthouse in Cuxhaven also doubled up as observation lookout base to keep tabs on traffic moving in and out of the Elbe estuary. In between is rather an interesting relic from the past, in the form of an information mast (seen in close-up *right*). This provided visual information for ships coming out of the River Elbe. Visitors are usually told it helped fishing boats by providing the latest information about the location of Barsch (bass) and herrings in the North Sea. Actually it gave the direction and strength of the wind near Borkum and Heligoland. Although radio has now replaced this old equipment, a local charity has purchased the structure and is keeping it operational.

Right:
In the foreground is the old minesweeper memorial as a poignant reminder that Cuxhaven was once an important naval base for this most dangerous work.

Chapter 2

Germany's Main Prewar Challenges

Denmark, Norway and Sweden

These countries were not considered as potential enemies in the prewar period and therefore very little was done to intercept their coded naval radio transmissions. Later, in 1940, when Germany invaded Denmark and Norway, the German Navy met only short-lived resistance from the military in these countries. Sweden was slightly different in that radio interception was put back on the list of priorities shortly before the end of the war, but very little progress was made with the breaking of its military codes.

Finland

Since Germany was on good terms with Finland and there were virtually no naval movements, no attempt was made to break into its coding systems.

France

The story of how a French officer successfully stole a working coding machine and sold it to the Germans for a high price through connections in Stockholm has featured in a variety of spy books in such a way that it makes one wonder whether there is any truth in it. Since the sources are difficult to trace and the majority of stories are so similar, it would suggest that many of the more dramatic details have come about by one author copying from another. However, it seems certain that a machine was sold to the Germans but this device was a prototype and it was not long before a considerable number of modifications to it were made. Therefore the 'lost' machine was never used operationally by the French Navy, but it did provide an insight into how their new system functioned and helped Germany in finding a means of cracking it. Sadly for the Germans, the French

Above: French battleship *Jean Bart* is seen at Casablanca in 1941 being inspected by members of the Disarmament Commission following the fall of France previous year. *Ian Allan Library*

Above: French battleship *Jean Bart* again, in Casablanca in November 1942, showing damage by shell fire and bombs caused by the US invasion of North Africa during Operation 'Torch'. *Ian Allan Library*

officer had enough wits to acquire a highly secret machine, but lacked the ability to hide what he had done and was stupid enough to go on an obvious shopping spree, spending much more than his meagre salary could allow. Consequently he was arrested, tried, sentenced and was no longer in a position to provide his German paymasters with any more assistance.

The French were certainly not complacent about the selection and use of their radio codes, and invested considerable effort in the creation of a foolproof system. Actually not just one but four basic coding structures were established for transmitting information to naval units. Each of these was highly complicated and for a long time all Germany could do was to classify intercepted messages according to the procedure they were thought to belong to. By the time the first was cracked, the code had already been changed, meaning Germany was, once more, left out in the cold. Nevertheless, understanding how the old system worked

made it easier to break into the new code. The long time and great effort invested in the exploration of these French systems paid dividends and all four were cracked before the war started, making it possible to read the majority of naval signals.

Soon after the beginning of the war, these codes were changed again and Germany had to start once more from the beginning. However, the basic routines and the ways in which the codes were put together remained virtually identical to the earlier, peacetime framework, making it relatively easy to gain a satisfactory enough insight into French radio traffic not to be surprised by its naval activities. After the fall of France, in June 1940, the Vichy Government agreed to use cipher systems known to the Germans and the few warships which escaped to Britain scrapped their existing broadcasting methods in order to adopt Royal Navy procedures. Therefore France ceased to be a challenge for the B-Dienst.

Great Britain

By the time the German Radio Monitoring Service re-established itself after World War 1, it discovered considerable changes had taken place in the use of British radio codes, making it much more difficult to read many of the new peacetime messages. What was more, a higher proportion of signals had been sent in plain language towards the end of the war than during the mid-1920s. This was partly explained by both sides having to employ poorly trained radio operators towards the end of the conflict, whereas afterwards the vast bureaucratic systems settled down with better educated staff. At first the B-Dienst thought Britain was using two different coding systems, but quickly came to the conclusion that one was probably more for shortening messages rather than concealing their meaning. It also became evident that a number of shipping lines devised their own coding methods for hiding sensitive information from the prying eyes of competitors.

Extensive research by the B-Dienst concluded Britain was using the International Merchant Navy Code together with a Naval Attachment for hiding vital information. The Royal Navy was transmitting a high proportion of messages in plain, readable text and used what was called the Royal Navy Administrative Code until the outbreak of war. This was based on a book which translated words and common phrases into a code. Half of the book then listed the codes to reveal their meaning. This, of course, had the disadvantage that each word was always represented by the same code and therefore it was not too long before Germany had built up a comprehensive collection of vocabulary to solve part of the problem. In addition to this, a large number of radio transmissions were made in what was called the Diplomatic Cipher, but most of this fell outside the jurisdiction of the German naval intelligence service.

The insight gained into the Royal Navy Administrative Code helped the B-Dienst considerably to break into the new Naval Cipher, which was introduced at the beginning of the war. In less than six months the B-Dienst was able to read an estimated third to a half of the intercepted messages. This code was used to transmit the run-of-the-mill material, but higher officers such Flag

Above: Looking across Horse Guards' Parade towards the Admiralty in London. The Citadel, or bunker, housing the wartime naval control centre, can be seen to the left. The tops of these buildings had a massive spider's web of an aerial until long after the war and could, no doubt, communicate with ships at sea a long distance away.

Above: Italian battleship *Littorio*. Completed in 1940, she was damaged during the Royal Navy's aerial attack on the Italian fleet at Taranto in November 1940. *IAL*

Officers, Commanders-in-Chief and the like used a different, more complicated code, which continued to baffle the B-Dienst. The ability to read the Naval Cipher provided the German Navy with a considerable advantage during the Norwegian Campaign of April 1940, but the course of events also made it clear to the Admiralty in London that the enemy had probably gained an insight into its coding system. Therefore steps were taken to change radio procedures.

In July/August 1940 Britain then changed the Administrative Code into Naval Code No 1 and the original Naval Cipher became Naval Cipher No 2. However, both these were so closely linked to the older systems, which they replaced, that the B-Dienst was given a strong impetus to break both of them, but this proved far more difficult than the first analyses suggested. A small amount of success was achieved in gaining some insight into Cipher No 2, but things looked bleak for the Germans for best part of a year until they had gained a considerable understanding of the code from the autumn of 1941. Naval Cipher No 4 replaced a large proportion of Cipher No 2 in January 1942 and this, strangely enough, made it possible to make major inroads in what was left of the existing Cipher No 2. By the following autumn, 1942, the Germans were also making some headway into deciphering Cipher No 4.

However, despite failing to gain a complete insight into the new codes, not all was lost in Germany. The prewar International Merchant Navy Code — the International Code and Naval Appendix — was replaced in January 1940 by the British Merchant Navy Code, which the B-Dienst cracked in less than three months. In May 1940, during the Norwegian Campaign, a complete code book was captured in Bergen, making it possible to read the majority of messages sent to convoys in the Atlantic. This new code remained in use until April 1942 when it was replaced by the Merchant Ships Code which was used in tandem with the Special Convoy Cipher — Naval Cipher No 3, introduced in June 1941. Germany actually managed to get hold of one of these new code books for the Merchant Ships Code before it was introduced, thus gaining a wonderful head start in the all-out important convoy war of the Atlantic. To make matters worse for Britain, the four-wheel Enigma machine was introduced to operational U-boats on 1 February 1942, meaning Bletchley Park was locked out until the end of the year, unable to gain easy clues about its new code having been compromised. The Convoy Cipher was abandoned towards the end of 1942/early 1943 because by that time suspicions that it had been compromised had grown enormously and the renewed understanding of German transmissions following the capture of the German four-wheel Enigma machine

Above:
The Italian cruiser *Bolzano*, shown here bomb-damaged in 1941. *IAL*

Right:
Only two years before the outbreak of war, the Soviet battleship *Marat*, in the foreground, and the German *Panzerschiff* (pocket battleship) *Admiral Scheer*, in the background, are photographed taking part in the Coronation Review in 1937. *IAL*

quickly confirmed that these fears were indeed true. The Merchant Ships Code continued but following changes to the code by the British at the end of 1943 and in 1944 it became much harder for the Germans to decipher it.

The new system for general radio communications, Naval Cipher No 5, introduced in June 1943, replaced the old Cipher Nos 3 and 4, both of which the Germans had managed to make good progress in decrypting, and this was never broken by the B-Dienst. For, joint British–Canadian–American communications in the Atlantic, this, incidentally, was replaced after a period of six months in late 1943 by a Combined Cipher. This was considerably more secure than the old code book system because it used a device, known as Typex (Type X), which was similar to the German Enigma machine.

Although the bulk of the Royal Navy and aircraft flying over the Atlantic used only a relatively small number of coding systems, more than 25 different ways of coding messages were actually used, meaning foreign cryptanalysts were faced with real challenges. What is more, the ability to read the Convoy Cipher may have given the German Navy an advantage by providing a 10–24-hour advance warning of convoy departures, but it still made it exceedingly difficult to follow them on the airwaves once they were underway because all manner of further secrets were injected. For example: 'Change to Course D at Point 5,' did not mean much to anyone who was not at the masters' briefing before departure.

The Royal Navy also used one-time cipher pads, and signals using these were impossible to break without obtaining a pad. At least one of these was captured shortly after the beginning of the war from a ship on its way back from Sweden with ball bearings. However, having laid their hands on the book, the Germans were still left out in the cold because the other party, which was supposed to have used it, had probably also been put out of action. The Radio Monitoring Service looked around for other ships which might be using the same code pad, but the records are obscure enough not to give any indication whether this was ever achieved.

Italy

Following World War 1, German interception of Italian naval radio traffic dwindled slowly until after Hitler came to power and Mussolini's neutral or even unfriendly stance caused the B-Dienst to become more deeply involved. However, the bristling hostility which was anticipated never developed and thus the entire Italian sphere of operation was slowly run down again. In fact, the relationship became exceedingly good and eventually led to deep and trusted co-operation between the two naval radio intercept departments. At first, Italy even supplied Germany with masses of signals picked up from the Mediterranean and this resulted in the two countries joining forces to decode them. This liaison was thorough enough for the B-Dienst to realise there was no

purpose in monitoring Italian radio, but this changed in September 1943, when the Allies invaded, the Italian government surrendered and the majority of the military changed sides to fight against Germany. Although the German Navy made a desperate effort to gain some insight into Italian radio systems, the majority of messages being broadcast from then on were in American or British code systems.

The Netherlands and Belgium

No large-scale attempts were made to intercept Dutch or Belgian naval radio or decipher their secret codes.

Poland

The Polish involvement in naval codes is still a major puzzle. They cracked Germany's highly complicated Enigma coding machine, but apparently never got around to devising their own impenetrable system. This is perhaps understandable, especially when once considers that their major base at Gdynia (later called Gotenhafen by the Germans) was a fishing village until the end of World War 1 and the facilities there were built exceedingly quickly to cover what was a very narrow stretch of coastline. In fact the only access Poland had to the Baltic was along this corridor separating East Prussia from the rest of Germany and therefore there was no great necessity to develop huge naval forces for defensive purposes.

Gaining an insight into the German Enigma system was indeed a fantastic achievement and it is sad that the Polish experts who accomplished this have received relatively little recognition. On the other hand, the German Navy was so well acquainted with the Polish cipher system that they used it to send messages to resistant groups between the start of their attack on 1 September 1939 and the last Polish capitulation, which resulted in a total cessation of naval radio traffic. The few Polish ships which made their way to Britain thereafter used Royal Navy ciphers, although there were times when the messages sent were worded in Polish rather than English.

The Soviet Union

Today it has largely been forgotten that Germany and Russia had a common frontier until the end of World War 1, although the immediate land on both sides was sparsely populated and there was very little interchange across it. The relationship between Nazi Germany and the communist Soviet Union was hardly amicable in the 1930s, but on 23 August 1939 they shocked the world by signing a non-aggression pact. This was rather significant as far as the B-Dienst was concerned because, according to Bonatz, it resulted in an official prohibition on intercepting or interfering with Soviet radio traffic. At the same time the Soviet section in the decoding department was shut down. Exactly what happened at this crucial period of time is difficult to reconstruct. Germany's eastern neighbour had two basic naval radio procedures and the B-Dienst had penetrated both of them. This effort was made more complicated by Russian naval units using their transmitters only occasionally, meaning the meat of the matter had to be scraped from a few far-flung and isolated bones. It is known that the German Navy continued to keep abreast with Russian codes after the prohibition, although it is not clear on what scale or on whose authority this was carried out. This will be discussed further in a later chapter.

Spain and Portugal

Although the Spanish Civil War is now usually pushed to the periphery of European history, it did present the German Navy with its first serious opportunity to break into Spanish operational codes. This was useful for the few ships stationed in or near Spanish coastal waters, but the breaking of the codes also helped the German government in obtaining a better insight into highly confusing situations on land, where news coverage was poor or even non-existent, and no one could be sure of what exactly was going on. However, both of the Spanish sides very quickly realised that their communications were providing the other with useful aids and therefore embarked upon quite complicated coding programmes. Germany may have had an excellent insight into Spanish coding systems used before the outbreak of the civil war but the cryptanalysts were quickly defeated by these new introductions. The Radio Monitoring Service succeeded in obtaining a spasmodic insight into what was going on, but never managed to crack the complete system until after the end of the civil war.

Portugal, on the other hand, was not considered to have been a threat to Germany and virtually no effort was made to intercept its radio transmissions or explore its naval codes.

Turkey

Although Germany took a deep interest in the radio traffic buzzing around the Black Sea, virtually nothing was done to break into the Turkish system until the last 10 months of the war and then only an exceedingly limited insight was gained. In any case, much of this was of little use to the German Navy since its activities in the Black Sea and in the eastern Mediterranean had already come to a halt by the time the first signals were decoded.

Above: The pocket battleship *Admiral Scheer*, with her rather solid-looking triangular control tower, is seen in southern waters during the Spanish Civil War. Although the pocket battleships were not conceived as merchant raiders, *Admiral Scheer* was to prove immensely successful during the war when used for commerce raiding.

Above: The captain of a large warship on the bridge with a speaking tube for shouting his orders to both helmsman and engine telegraph operator. To the right is a sailor with heavy headsets and a large mouthpiece, which is hidden from view, for transmitting other information. Electric telephones had started to make communications throughout warships much faster and could be used in noisy locations where speaking tubes were impractical.

USA

Neither the German government nor the Navy showed a great deal of interest in intercepting American radio messages until the fateful attack on Pearl Harbor in December 1941 brought a drastic change in attitude. Therefore it was the beginning of 1942 before the Radio Monitoring Service embarked upon a systematic analysis of the American systems. It was quickly discovered that two main codes were in use. One of these was based on what appeared to have been some mechanical device, probably a circular slide rule type of gadget. The other was found to be exceptionally simple and Heinz Bonatz (head of the B-Dienst) said the United States could have saved itself the trouble of coding the messages at all and

might just as well have sent them in plain language. In fact, this was so undemanding that the men aboard the pocket battleship *Admiral Scheer* managed to read many signals while their ship was sailing down the Atlantic during their long cruise into southern waters in the autumn of 1940.

However, things soon became more complicated. Although the Germans could decrypt much of the British Naval Cipher No 3 (the Convoy Cipher), introduced in June 1941 to cover joint Allied convoy transmissions, the introduction towards the end of 1943/early 1944 of the Combined British–Canadian–American Cipher System, based on the Typex (Type X) machine, made it virtually impossible for Germany to break into the system.

Chapter 3
The New, Bigger Departments

By the time World War 2 started, the coastal radio stations with direction finders, mentioned in the first chapter, were fully operational, passing on a considerable volume of messages. The weak link in this interception process was in the deciphering department at headquarters in Berlin, which still had not reached the size laid down in the plans conceived in 1935. Therefore, excessive pressure fell on the expertise of the regional centres to sift messages before passing them on for decoding. However, this weakness faded rapidly once the war started because the flow of naval messages from the east came to a standstill, meaning it was possible to direct the limited resources at what were thought to be the most profitable French and British signals.

In any case, the main emphasis shifted very quickly from deciphering messages to recruitment and training of new staff. This problem was made a little easier by the war having put a number of suitable people out of work. For example, businessmen with good language skills from import and export firms suddenly found their daily activities curtailed and it was not long before such people were enticed to join the code-breaking departments. Academics were also sought, but these had to be carefully selected because a high proportion of them had little experience with the practicalities of life and they easily allowed themselves to become bogged down with theoretical explorations, without finding a practical solution to their problems. Training these people was indeed most difficult. There were simply no teachers and the few experts with the right knowledge were required in the more important jobs of cracking codes. So, to get over this problem, the Navy started looking for alert people with good skills in at least one foreign language. Ideally, these new recruits also had to have some knowledge of ships and shipping, or even yachting and sailing. Once through the selection procedure, they were shown what to do, how to get on with it and then they were handed some simple tasks to sort out for themselves. Those who learned quickly were promoted; those who coped reasonably well were left to plod on; those with no visible aptitude for the laborious tasks were pushed into other less taxing avenues.

Above: U393 making fast in Kiel with ObltzS Alfred Radermacher holding the essential megaphone for shouting orders to the crew working on the upper deck. The white symbol to the left of the horseshoe-shaped lifebelt is an identification mark for training, suggesting this picture was taken before the boat left for its first operational voyage. Radermacher is rather an interesting character: he started his career as action helmsman in *U5* and thus was one of the first men to serve in U-boats before the outbreak of World War 2 and from there worked his way up from the lowest sailor rank to officer and then became a commander. He had the good fortune to survive the war

Above: A group of boys from the Hitler Youth being given some sea-going experience aboard a warship with an opportunity to use their semaphore skills. Semaphore remained an essential communication method throughout World War 2.

The next problem to arise was that the best of these new recruits were considerably sharper, quicker and more able than men drawn from the Navy, making it necessary to promote them to key positions above existing naval officers. This, of course, was unheard of. After all, naval officers considered themselves to be direct descendants of God and there was no way the bureaucratic system of the time could allow a civilian, the lowest form of life, to tell an officer what to do. This was solved by first making the likely candidates Reserve Officers and then placing them in the critical positions as heads of sections. This actually worked quite well, although the Navy did not waive its recruitment and training rules. Therefore, these key people vanished from the scene while they attended officer training establishments to complete the necessary courses. Warrant officers were also considered for special rapid promotion. Although the temporary absence of such people was a nuisance to the Radio Monitoring Service, the staff there could draw some comfort from training having been reduced to the barest minimum and, on top of this, it was sometimes possible to get around the

system, allowing the cryptanalysts to miss irrelevant parts of the programme. Nevertheless, despite their lack of military drill, the service these people provided was considerably more valuable than what might have been achieved, had they been shunted into some ordinary fighting unit. The officers of the Supreme Naval Command were more than satisfied with their new code breakers. On the whole they provided unexpectedly excellent results.

This recruitment system worked well enough to increase the numbers of staff at the Radio Monitoring Service's headquarters in Berlin from an initial figure well below the earlier projected 120 to about 1,000, and later almost 6,000 people became involved with naval code breaking and its associated intelligence. It may be interesting to compare this figure with Bletchley Park in England, which employed about 10,000–12,000 people later in the war to deal with all of its responsibilities, not just German naval matters. The German process was still expanding when, early in 1942, the occasional lectures and practical sessions to help new recruits were replaced with a six-week induction course to teach the basics of

Above: Balancing high up on a ship to send semaphore messages could be quite tricky and the majority of small boats preferred to use Morse lamps. These had a sighting tube to align them with the target, while a Morse key switched the bulb on and off. Here Oberfunkmaat Horenburg is using a signal lamp aboard *U407*.

Above: Semaphore, or floor cloth waving as the German Navy called it, was often used to transmit messages during daylight, while a searchlight sending Morse was used at night.

Above: U393 with Morse lamp in action.

code breaking and to help people fit into their new roles within a close-knit community, where determination, accuracy, persistence and teamwork were of vital importance. Some judgement of the department's capacity can be gained when one considers that on average 3,000 messages arrived each day at the decoding centre. These, of course, had already been sorted into types and graded in urgency, but the code breakers were still faced with a mammoth task.

Efficient and rapid expansion on all fronts was a significant factor in the B-Dienst's success. Six years earlier, the main out-stations boasted of one, two or three telex machines and now they had several rooms accommodating up to 50 of these devices. These generated enough noise to make conversation near them impossible, making it necessary to shout or go into a different room when discussions had to take place. In addition to this telex traffic, there was also a daily air mail courier service connecting the regional headquarters with Berlin, so the flow of information was indeed on a most significant scale and no expense was spared to move as quickly as possible. The whole system reached its peak early in 1943 and then remained at that high level until the Allied D-Day invasion of Normandy, after which bases in France had gradually to be abandoned. Of course, the shrinking of the German code-breaking system had begun earlier, during the first few months of 1943, when the Army suffered heavy defeats in Russia, but this hardly affected the naval Radio Monitoring Service.

Early in 1942 the navy's Radio Monitoring Service consisted of the following main departments (see Appendix I for a diagram showing how the Radio Monitoring Service was incorporated into the organisation of naval intelligence):

1. The main Evaluation and Intelligence Centre.
2. Department West I, responsible for decoding British signals.
3. Department West II, decoding American signals.
4. Department East, dealing with Russian matters.
5. Cipher School and Training Department.

However, this system was already near bursting point and it was not long before a reorganisation programme changed the entire setup by pruning off various areas of responsibility. For example, the sections dealing with the west were further divided to produce a new department responsible for convoys and sea communications; there was a department specialising in the checking of all German naval ciphers including security matters relating to the Enigma machine; a department responsible for technical matters relating to the radio equipment being used; another one dealing solely with personnel; as well as a special evaluation service for urgent messages.

This setup worked exceedingly well, not only supplying a vast flow of essential information but also getting it to the appropriate sea commanders at the right

A radio intercept room reconstructed by David White and now on display at Bletchley Park, showing the type of equipment which was used during World War 2.

Above: The main control tower of the pocket battleship *Admiral Graf Spee* with several searchlights visible. Although these were primarily intended for night-time illumination of targets, they also had shutters and could be used to transmit visual Morse messages over considerable distances, as long as visibility permitted. Such massive lamps were powered by arc lights, rather than light bulbs, and these took some time to ignite; therefore they could not be switched on and off quickly for sending Morse messages and were fitted with a shutter system instead.

time. Of course, as has always been the case, sea-going officers usually complained, saying the information arrived too late to act upon, but such gripes were common to all military services of all sides. The weak link in the network appears to have been between the Radio Monitoring Service and the men who gave the orders at sea. In Britain this was overcome by having a special intelligence team to translate the raw messages into easily comprehensible instructions. For example, decoded naval messages were sorted by experts at Bletchley Park and then this material went on to the Operational Intelligence Centre at the Admiralty in London. There, experts translated this information into manageable bites before it was transmitted on to the relevant commanders. At the same time, it was often necessary to rewrite the data to hide its origin. Only the highest ranking sea-going officers and a few of their staff knew about the existence of Bletchley Park or what was going on there.

This crucial link was missing in Germany. Instead of supplying commanders at the front with pre-digested data, they were often given raw facts and these appeared in quantities vast enough to overwhelm the recipients. After the war, many of them realised they did not have enough time to cope with the masses of material flowing in. This was not so much of a problem aboard large ships, where officers could concentrate on their immediate situation and what was likely to influence them in the near future, but it became a stumbling block for many land-based command centres, especially the all-important U-boat Command which had both to control everyday operations and make longer-term plans. The staff there suffered considerably from this oversupply of undigested intelligence and this was made worse as the war progressed. Difficulties at sea, caused by Britain being able to read the secret Enigma code, resulted in several spy hunts, which in turn led to a reduction in the number of people who were acquainted with current U-boat activities. This gave rise to a state of affairs where men found each day too short for coping with their immediate operational problems. They were left mentally and physically exhausted, making it

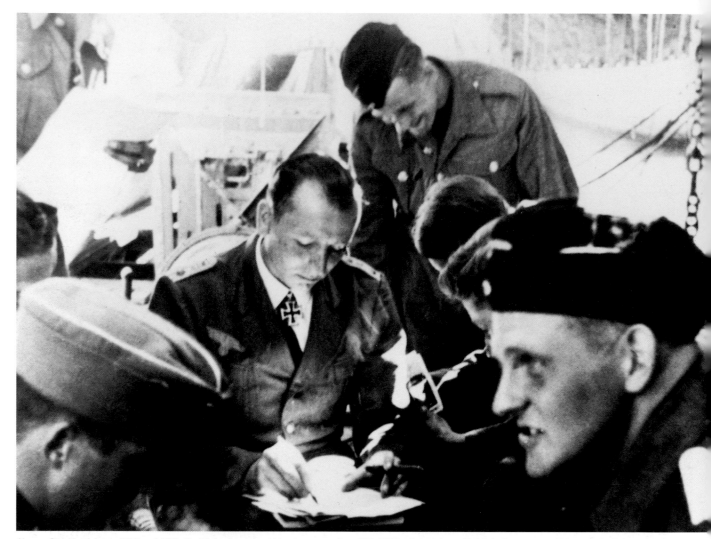

Above: Otto Kretschmer (*U23* and *U99*), the highest scoring U-boat commander of World War 2, wearing a Knight's Cross around his neck, in the centre of the photograph. He was nicknamed 'Silent Otto' because he rarely used his radio. Many U-boat commanders were under the impression (correctly) that the position of their transmissions could be detected by British radio direction finders and therefore refused to broadcast unless their position had been revealed by the opposition. The man in the foreground, towards the right, could be Erich Topp, commander of *U57, U552, U3010, U2513* and of the 27th U-Flotilla.

exceedingly difficult to understand the significance of many intercepted messages. This became so bad that vital messages and important clues were overlooked merely because there were not enough people to chew through the material being provided by the Radio Monitoring Service.

Germany made the big mistake of thinking much of this highly sensitive intelligence work should be carried out by men with sea-going experience. In fact the majority of the staff at U-boat headquarters were former submarine commanders who were Knights of the Iron Cross. By contrast, Britain realised that providing men with recent fighting experience was not the answer to the problem and recruited a large number of technical experts to analyse the highly specialised information.

The technological side of the intelligence game was considerably easier to cope with than the manpower issue and generally the progress in this field was more than satisfactory. As has already been said, the entire radio

system had been created shortly before the beginning of the war and the necessary land lines were in position, and tried and tested by 1939. The stations had the latest in specially designed radios for picking up foreign broadcasts, accurate and fairly easy to operate radio direction finders and direct telephone connections with one another. This meant it was no longer necessary to copy a signal and write the bearing from which it came on paper to be transmitted to a central station where the exact position was worked out. It was a case of one operator telling another, a long way away, about the signal he was receiving and almost instantly getting the other station's bearing on that source. Although much of this radio gear received slight modifications as the war progressed, it remained basically the same throughout and an operator from the early days would easily have felt at home with the more modern sets installed later in the war. In fact, this simplicity made it easy to duplicate radio direction finding and intercept stations in

Above: Obermaschinist Gerhard Leissner holding a microphone for Kptlt Friedrich Marks aboard *U376*. This radio broadcasting microphone was of a modern, small variety. A few years earlier such devices would have been much bigger.

Right:
U10 with an early, circular radio direction finder aerial attached to the outside of the conning tower. These were added as an afterthought, but did allow the aerial to be moved from side to side. The boat had to sail in a circle if it wished to home in on transmissions coming from astern. These devices were fitted at a time when no one was really sure how they should be used and they were quickly improved to provide a better service. The aerial intake wire, connecting the large jumping wires with the radio room, can be seen to the right of the bottom of the loop, while there is a fog horn under the eagle's wing.

Above: U48, the most successful U-boat of World War 2, with Obersteuermann (Navigator) Willi Kronenbitter on the left and the commander, Kptlt Herbert Schultze, on the right. The retractable radio direction finder loop is prominent.

Denmark, Norway, Holland, Belgium, France and other countries during the war. The most successful equipment was simply copied, set up in favourable locations and connected with secure land lines to a central control room. This worked well and much of the expansion in foreign countries ran without noteworthy problems and, as a bonus, it was possible to get even clearer reception on some far-off stations than from the bases at home. Indeed, operators could hear transmitters which could not be picked up from within the frontiers of the Reich.

There were plans for building a deciphering machine similar to the Bombes and Colossus computers used at Bletchley Park, but naval resources did not stretch as far as putting these ideas into practice and the industrial firms capable of making such equipment were fully occupied with other, supposedly more important, wartime tasks. Ideas and designs were not the major stumbling block. The biggest problem was finding a way of proving that the finished product would actually do the job. Anyway, such ambitious projects may have been thought about and discussed, but none of them ever got off the ground. The only aid used by the deciphering and intelligence departments was a punch card type of calculator-cum-sorting-machine, which was introduced towards the end of 1942. Each card, with holes in the appropriate places, was drawn automatically into the machine, read and processed to help with a variety of statistical tasks as well as sorting or searching for common denominators in a mass of otherwise unmanageable data. Each machine probably read about 10,000 cards per hour, an incredibly slow performance when compared with modern computers, but the time required for people to sort through such a mass of often confusing data was enormous compared with the performance of the machine. Yet it is strange that these devices were first used by the B-Dienst only as late as the end of 1942. After all, the system on which they were based had been invented by an American, Herman Hollerith, in the late 19th century. Hollerith machines were well known to businessmen and statisticians around the world well before World War 2 and had been used by the American military since at least the 1930s.

Right:
The retractable radio direction finder loop aboard *U31*. The hatband with the flotilla name *Saltzwedel* worn by the man on the left indicates this picture was taken before the war. Binoculars could be butted onto the special sunglasses he is wearing.

Chapter 4
The Lurch into Action: the B-Dienst Finds its Feet

The signal 'Total Germany' which announced Britain's declaration of war was intercepted by the B-Dienst at 11.17 hours on 3 September 1939, and naturally came as no surprise to Berlin. The B-Dienst had been deciphering all manner of war preparations being broadcast to both the Royal and Merchant Navies since before the beginning of August. This inflated flow of information quickly changed into a slow trickle. The head of the B-Dienst, Heinz Bonatz, later stated that he and his men were surprised to find that much of the vital war news that was still being broadcast in plain language, even after the outbreak of hostilities. This comment is rather strange as he must have known that the British merchant ships were following an international agreement which made it necessary for warring nations to give ample warning of any obstructions they placed in sea lanes, whether these were in territorial waters or not. As a result, announcements of new shipping routes and reports of the blocking of existing shipping lanes with net and mine barrages were regularly repeated for several days. Yet the B-Dienst apparently wondered whether this was some type of propaganda aimed at keeping German forces away from the British coast, rather than being intended to help small ships which did not have full-time radio operators. It was only in January 1940 that the British introduced the Merchant Navy Code to replace the International Code and Naval Appendix.

The other unexpected development was that nothing of great moment happened at sea. Some in Germany had even expected the Home Fleet to appear in the German Bight to challenge not only its commercial traffic but also the coastal towns. The Royal Navy seemed to withdraw into mysterious locations, leaving the obvious anchorages empty, or, at least, the radio rooms of ships in those locations shut down. This was quite unsettling for the B-Dienst, with radio operators initially under the impression that they were missing the bulk of the broadcasts. Checks were made on equipment, to see whether it was functioning properly, and the out-of-the-way corners of the airwaves searched, in case the British had found new frequencies for their regular channels. The meaning of the silence in the ether had to be confirmed by visual sightings and the field of view from even the tallest lighthouses along the low German coast was only 50 miles or so on the

few exceptionally clear days. Ideally, the Radio Monitoring Service wanted to send out reconnaissance aircraft to confirm whether its suspicions were correct, but the few aircraft under naval jurisdiction either did not have the range or they were needed for more important tasks elsewhere. Therefore the small volume of supporting photographs was slow in coming.

Lack of information was also an issue during the attack on Poland. Only a few antiquated ships or those with mechanical faults were found in harbour and intelligent guesswork was necessary to find the rest. The B-Dienst was hardly in a position to help. The Polish Navy used its radios for sending only occasional messages, making it difficult to collect intercepts and impossible for direction finders to provide an accurate overall picture of where the ships were. However, on land the German forces managed to cut off Poland's ports so swiftly that the few ships at sea were left in a dire predicament, without support. It quickly became clear there would be no great naval conflict in the Baltic and on 11 September, the B-Dienst obtained the necessary confirmation that Polish naval units at sea with sufficient fuel were making their way to Britain while others were seeking refuge in neutral Swedish waters.

It did not take long before the Radio Monitoring Service confirmed that Britain was using its advantageous geographical location to blockade the northern extremities of the North Sea. The B-Dienst's reports that a large number of aircraft and ships were operating in this area were soon confirmed by U-boats, who found passing through this cordon to and from the Atlantic rather uncomfortable. However, the German merchant ships which happened to be at sea when the war began found the situation even trickier. Many were captured far from home; others sought internment in neutral ports; some were caught trying to pass the British blockade; and the few which got home mostly did so by creeping along the Norwegian coast.

Not having the resources to strike at the British patrols, the German Navy stewed in its own juice for some time until someone suggested it might be possible to launch a large-scale radio deception exercise. Consequently a flood of bogus orders, modifications of earlier instructions and all manner of viable information were broadcast from a number of radio transmitters. Even ships being repaired in port with partly working

Above: U35 with extended radio direction finder and 88mm quick firing gun in front of the conning tower. The object in the foreground at deck level is a rescue buoy with a flashing light, which could be released from the inside during an emergency.

Above: The circular radio direction finder aerial of a U-boat retracted inside its housing in the conning tower wall. This looks very much like a modification added after the conning tower had been built, but in later boats the slot was designed as an integral part of the boat. The circular object to the right of the man is a speaking tube connecting the duty officer with the helmsman and engine telegraphs.

equipment were drawn into the game and, very much to the German Navy's surprise, Britain reacted by increasing air cover in the appropriate areas and ordering the Home Fleet to sea. This did not alleviate the original problem, but proved beyond doubt that Britain was taking note of German signals.

There were also some strange incidents, such as an aircraft reporting the pocket battleship *Admiral Scheer* off Heligoland while she was lying in a repair berth in Wilhelmshaven. The Luftwaffe got as far as bouncing a bomb off the battlecruiser *Hood* and obtaining a near miss on the aircraft carrier *Ark Royal*, but very little other damage was done. However, the deception exercise did prove to the Radio Monitoring Service that something more critical might be attempted at a later date. The deception and other events also proved that some British personnel were just as inexperienced as their German counterparts. There were even occasions when British ships as large as cruisers reported sighting enemy aircraft but forgot to give their own positions.

In this way the Royal Navy and the Kriegsmarine stumbled blindly into the autumn of 1939, almost as if playing a game of football with both sides either blindfolded or at best wearing frosted glass goggles to restrict their field of vision. In September 1939, for example, the Admiralty in London guessed there might be some German surface raiders at sea, but did not know how many or where they were likely to be. Consequently, the two pocket battleships, *Admiral Graf Spee* (KptzS Hans Langsdorff) in the South Atlantic and *Deutschland* (KptzS Paul Wenneker) in the north, succeeded in disposing of several ships without the Admiralty knowing exactly what was going on. The extensive radio traffic which followed when the raiders' presence became known also benefited Germany inasmuch as it showed how violently Britain could react once the Admiralty had the slightest whiff of any movement on the high seas. Therefore, Germany made an even more determined effort to hide all indications of warship movements.

Getting into the Atlantic was made considerably easier for German raiders by *U47's* (Kptlt Günther Prien) penetration into Scapa Flow during the night of 13/14 October 1939, when the battleship *Royal Oak* was sunk. As a result, the big ships of the British Home Fleet were moved to safer anchorages on the west coast of Scotland, where they were further from the routes in and out of the North Sea. Shortly after *U47's* attack there were indications of big ships moving west and it was not long before the B-Dienst came to believe they were making for Loch Ewe. The probable use of this sea loch as a major anchorage instead of Scapa Flow was later confirmed by an unusually large number of signals from the area.

In November 1939 the battlecruisers *Gneisenau* (KptzS Erich Förste) and *Scharnhorst* (KptzS Kurt Caesar Hoffmann), at that time Germany's most powerful ships, broke through the narrows between Scotland and Norway during appallingly bad weather to commence a raid against merchant traffic in order to take pressure off *Admiral Graf Spee*. The Admiralty in London had no idea about the whereabouts of the two elusive sisters and didn't even guess they might be at large in the North Atlantic. Apparently, even the first sighting reports were not believed and taken to be a misidentification. The first indication of them being at sea was transmitted a few minutes before 16.00 hours on 23 November 1939, when the armed merchant cruiser *Rawalpindi*, under Captain E. C. Kennedy, sighted a warship emerging out of the mists at a range of about four miles. This was taken to be British at first, but it was not long before Kennedy identified it as a German battlecruiser. At this point two different versions of the story appear. First, the official British account explains how Kennedy corrected himself a few minutes later, saying the intruder was the pocket battleship *Deutschland*. Captain Stephen Roskill, in his British official history, *The War at Sea*, gave details of how easy it would have been for Kennedy to be confused into making such a wrong identification. He pointed out that *Deutschland* was known to have been in the North Atlantic and looked very similar to both *Scharnhorst* and *Gneisenau*. Such a remark may have held water in the early 1950s, when he was writing his account and his readers had not seen many photos of the ships, but it looks rather dubious today. There were in fact considerable differences between *Deutschland's* small pocket battleship silhouette and that of the *Scharnhorst*, then one of the two biggest ships in the

Above: The Royal Navy battleship HMS *Royal Oak* which was sunk by *U47* whilst in the British Home Fleet's anchorage in Scapa Flow in October 1939. *IAL*

Left and above: The massive masts of the radio station near Daventry (England), which can be seen from the M1 motorway, photographed in the year 2002. This huge complex played a significant role in the development of radar, being the transmitter for the first serious radio detection experiments. During World War 2 it became a major broadcasting base for all manner of official communications and made many of the transmissions which were intercepted by the German Monitoring Service.

Above: The 16,697grt British passenger ship *Rawalpindi* in Shanghai during 1938. She was later converted to become an armed merchant cruiser and used to escort a convoy when she encountered the battlecruiser *Scharnhorst*. She was sunk in a matter of a few minutes by *Scharnhorst*, which was able to stay outside the effective range of *Rawalpindi's* inferior armament.

German Navy. The *Deutschland* had only one forward gun turret and a relatively low superstructure, while the *Scharnhorst* had two such turrets on the bows, with quite a solid and highly imposing superstructure. Would someone with Captain Kennedy's experience have mistaken one for the other? It is possible, but seems highly unlikely.

Right: A dramatic painting, dating from 1940, of the attack on the *Rawalpindi* by the Scharnhorst. *IAL*

The second interesting version of this story comes from German intercept stations. Apparently the name '*Deutschland*' was transmitted in plain language, not in the code being used by *Rawalpindi*. In addition to this, there are strong indications in German records to suggest this second message came from a different transmitter, in a different location from the one which

sent the earlier sighting report. Therefore, German analysts have put forward the theory that the second message could have been transmitted by the Admiralty in London, telling its ships that the enemy vessel Kennedy had reported was the smaller *Deutschland*, rather than a bigger battlecruiser. But why hide this apparently insignificant error? Possibly, during the early 1950s, it was still inappropriate to admit such a drastic mistake had been made in Whitehall and that the naval authorities there had no clue as to what was going on in the North Atlantic nor had any idea about the dispositions of German naval units.

Whatever, more humiliation was to follow. *Rawalpindi* was sunk quickly by *Scharnhorst's* superior armament. The Germans were still picking up survivors when the cruiser *Newcastle* appeared, but allowed the Germans to vanish into a patch of bad visibility and quietly return home soon after. From then on the radio waves erupted into activity, telling the B-Dienst that a force of considerable size was being assembled to challenge the battlecruiser. Reports from survivors, as well as virtually simultaneous sightings at different locations, suggested that not one but two similar ships were at sea. Since *Scharnhorst* and *Gneisenau* were almost identical, it was not too difficult to guess who they were. This news created considerable embarrassment in London, where stalwart admirals were maintaining *Rawalpindi* had been sunk as a result of accidentally running into a homeward-bound pocket battleship. The German Naval War Staff was delighted. Twice in two months it had succeeded in drawing the imposing British Home Fleet into the Atlantic and the B-Dienst was over the moon at having been able to supply a running commentary of the events as they developed.

There were times when the B-Dienst was able to provide almost simultaneous reports while the action was still unfolding. For example, on 21 November 1939 it intercepted a signal saying the cruiser *Belfast* had run onto a mine. This was known to have been laid a few days earlier by *U21* under Kptlt Fritz Frauenheim, but there were no immediate indications as to whether *Belfast* had been damaged or not. Then, shortly afterwards the B-Dienst decoded an in itself innocuous signal, giving details of leave for the *Belfast's* crew. Two weeks had been allocated. Half of the men were going to be away for the first week, while the other half were going home for the second. This then suggested to the B-Dienst that the damage was sufficient to force the ship into dock and put it out of action for at least a couple of weeks. (In fact, *Belfast* was out of action for two years.)

Some commanders were far more economical with the information they allowed to be broadcast, making it difficult to speculate what might be afoot. To give just one example, the flagship of the Home Fleet, the battleship *Nelson*, ran onto a mine while entering Loch Ewe on 4 December 1939. This had been laid a few days earlier

by *U31* under Kptlt Johannes Habekost. However, the ether remained silent and Germany had no way of finding out that anything untoward had happened. Possibly, had this happened in reverse and the ship stopped suddenly on her way out, the B-Dienst might have been able to draw some inferences, but on this occasion all Germany knew was that the flagship had arrived in Loch Ewe. A signal intercepted a few days later, saying *Nelson* was going south to Portsmouth, did not provide any significant clues either. It was only when Germany realised the Commander-in-Chief of the Home Fleet was transferring his flag to the battlecruiser *Hood* that the B-Dienst guessed something untoward could have happened. After all, why should the C-in-C suddenly move from one ship to another? Of course, the B-Dienst knew a U-boat had been laying mines, but that had taken place some weeks earlier and tying the signal of *Nelson* going south with a mine was very difficult. Situations in which German units reported attacking something were easier to follow because such obvious clues put the radio intercept stations on alert to start searching the airwaves for possibly revealing transmissions from the enemy but this *Nelson* incident is a good example of how difficult it was to connect the various messages which appeared out of the blue and where there was no obvious clue as to why they had been transmitted.

An incident on 28 December 1939 in which the battleship *Barham* was torpedoed by *U30* under Kptlt Fritz-Julius Lemp is a good example of how well the B-Dienst could keep tabs on events when the Royal Navy obliged by transmitting the necessary pointers. Like the mine incidents, there was no communication from *U30* and the B-Dienst did not even know the U-boat was prowling so close to the British coast. Lemp was frightened by the power of land-based radio direction finders and concentrated on extricating himself from a difficult predicament, rather than using the radio to tell the U-boat Command what he had just done. Consequently, the first clue of something out of the ordinary happening came from the British side, when a sudden flow of urgent operational signals interrupted the silence in the airwaves. Although there were a good number of messages, the B-Dienst did not immediately make a connection between a U-boat attack and the battleship. It was not until a short time later, when the 3rd Destroyer Flotilla was ordered to assist, that it guessed the damage had probably not been caused by a mine and that the attacker was still at large. *Barham's* signal, saying she was making for the Clyde at 12 knots indicated some damage had occurred, otherwise a battleship would likely be moving faster. However, at this stage, the B-Dienst still had no definite clue about the cause of the problem and the likelihood of *Barham* having run onto a mine, like the *Belfast* and *Nelson*, had to remain as an option. The intercepted signal said the bows had dropped some 9 feet (2.5 metres) in the water, which suggested significant damage had been inflicted, but still did not provide positive evidence as to the cause. Quite a while later, long after a detailed damage report had been submitted, a general U-boat warning was broadcast to all ships in the area. Even at that stage, the B-Dienst still could not determine which submarine might have been responsible, without specifically asking its operations room. Daily position reports were not recorded until the autumn of the following year.

By the end of 1939, the B-Dienst had collected sufficient information for patterns to emerge and for the meaning of various code names to become understandable. For example, after the sinking of the *Royal Oak* in Scapa Flow, 'Port A' cropped up frequently enough to suggest this had become an alternative anchorage, but finding the actual location was most difficult. In the end, after enough clues had accumulated, the 'A' seemed highly likely to refer to Aultbea, a tiny crofting community on the east side of Loch Ewe. The gathered information like this was comprehensive enough for the B-Dienst to provide a detailed and fairly accurate list of where Royal Navy ships were located. This was more than useful at the time, especially as the main emphasis was still on the employment of large surface ships, rather than on the submarine war. The German High Command had great expectations of employing its raiders in all-out battles against British merchant shipping, hoping that these might annihilate an entire convoy during one short, swift action.

At this stage of the war, a variety of ideas were circulating in naval circles about the value of the Radio Monitoring Service. On the one hand, there were those who put it on a par with fortune tellers and thought it would be best to plough on without it. On the other, there were a good number of planners who found the information most valuable, but despite this the B-Dienst still had to establish itself as a significant contributor if it was going to make a significant impact on the outcome of the war at sea. This was not easy, especially as some of the naval hierarchy were under the impression the war would end fairly soon, making it pointless to invest too much in long-term intelligence. The Radio Monitoring Service itself was more than content with the information it was providing and pleased at having been able to prove the sceptics wrong on many occasions. The conversion from the earlier peacetime role to becoming a key contributor to the war effort had gone considerably better than expected, but getting this recognised was not easy. Earlier prophecies of Britain producing a series of impenetrable wartime codes had been proved to be fallacious, and the B-Dienst demonstrated it was not only possible to understand British codes, but this could be done quickly enough to be of immediate operational value. Even if this was not achieved all the time, the piles of information collected about the enemy were enormous and contained enough substance for intelligence officers to draw significant conclusions.

Sadly, because the B-Dienst's performance was allowed to slide into oblivion after the war without proper evaluation on either the German or the British side, it is now difficult to reconstruct how some of the events were actually unravelled at the time or why radio monitors took such an especially deep interest in some apparently insignificant events. What is more, there are numerous incidents where it is difficult to reconstruct exactly how much the B-Dienst did know about them. One such interesting action took place early in 1940 when the British submarines *Undine* (Lt-Cdr Jackson), *Seahorse* (Lt Dawson) and *Starfish* (Lt Turner) ventured into the German Bight to be attacked and sunk on 6, 7 and 9 January respectively. Although hard evidence appears to be non-existent, the B-Dienst seems to have had prior warning and minesweepers were hurriedly sent out to locate them. *Seahorse* was depth-charged to disappear with all hands; *Starfish* was blown to the surface, allowing the crew to be saved while the boat was scuttled; *Undine* was forced to the surface as well and Korvettenkapitän (Korvkpt) Fritz Petzel, together with some other men, managed to get on board amidst a confusing situation to salvage a variety of code books from the radio room. Petzel later became commander of the 12th Minesweeper Flotilla, which had captured *Undine*, and even served with the specialised minesweeping flotilla on the River Danube, but was killed in action on 9 November 1941. The auxiliary minesweepers, *M1201*, *M1204* and *M1207*, which had surrounded *Undine*, made a desperate effort to attach a tow rope, but there were no submarine experts at hand and it was not long before she dropped away into the depths.

The B-Dienst's staff were delighted with the captured material from *Undine* because it confirmed that the majority of their predictions had been correct. In a way they were also disappointed that the books did not yield a great deal of new information, but the positive verification of their efforts was certainly much appreciated.

Another noteworthy B-Dienst achievement came early in 1940 when the department intercepted a fairly accurate description of the German supply ship *Altmark* with the remark she was almost certainly back in Germany. The reason for publishing this information was probably to tidy up earlier details saying *Altmark* had been in the South Atlantic with the pocket battleship *Admiral Graf Spee*. The description had then been well advertised in the hope that some passing ship might provide a clue to the raider's whereabouts. *Altmark* in fact was still at sea, attempting to run the blockade back to Germany, when this signal was intercepted, so the B-Dienst was pleased to pass on such details which could only help the supply ship. However, the joy was short-lived. Shortly after midday on 12 February 1940, news was broadcast of such a ship having been sighted on a southerly course near Tromsö in Norway. The results were incredible, almost as if a volcano had just erupted, making it difficult for German intercept stations to keep pace with the rapid flow of messages coming from all manner of unlikely places, highlighting Britain's interest in the ship.

This initial outburst was still subsiding when the B-Dienst detected no less than seven cruisers leaving Rosyth in Scotland. Whether these had any connection with *Altmark* was not known at the time, but one of them, HMS *Penelope*, reported colliding with an unidentified object and immediately made her way back. Every Royal Navy ship knew this could not become a straightforward action of one ship gunning another into oblivion. Cunning and daring was going to play a vital role if the ship was going to be apprehended. The B-Dienst followed the chain of events quite easily, though Germany's comparative weakness at sea meant that little could be done to block the British moves. The department was able to report how the British destroyer *Cossack* breached Norwegian neutrality to board the *Altmark* inside Norwegian territorial waters and how a number of Norwegian torpedo boats made little or no effort to defend their realm. The boarding party from the *Cossack* freed the prisoners being held aboard the ship (which was itself a breach of Norwegian neutrality).

The *Altmark* incident had hardly been digested when the B-Dienst set alarm bells ringing inside the Supreme Naval Command. The first sign of potential trouble came with an increase in radio traffic around the north of Scotland and then there followed evidence of several ships being refuelled at Scapa Flow. Such a conglomeration of heavy warships had not been assembled since a few months earlier, when the Royal Navy tried to bring *Scharnhorst* and *Gneisenau* to battle. Something appeared to be going on, but despite all efforts, no definite clues could be squeezed out of the ether. There were no major German ships at large to warrant

such panic, so whatever was causing the unrest had to have been initiated by the British side. To make matters worse, the Royal Navy was doing something to make deciphering more difficult and only a few sections of the messages could be converted into recognisable words. However, these brief passages included phrases such as 'troops at 48 hour standby' and 'transfer troops', all pointing to a landing of some sort, but providing no clue as to where this might be taking place. At first it was thought this could be a large-scale exercise or even a deliberate deception game, but as more messages poured

Right: The Royal Navy battleship HMS *Rodney*, with the battleship HMS *Barham* astern, at firing practice. The *Rodney* led the British naval force despatched to Norway to attempt to halt the German invasion. *IAL*

Above: The British destroyer *Glowworm* which was sunk in the Norway campaign after taking on the German heavy cruiser *Admiral Hipper*. She went down with most of her crew after deliberately ramming the *Hipper*. The captain of the *Glowworm*, Lieutenant Commander Gerald Roope, was awarded a posthumous VC for the action. *IAL*

Above: A German minesweeper in Oslo harbour in 1940 following Germany's successful invasion of Norway. *IAL*

Above: Despite many claims to the contrary, the prototype pocket battleship *Deutschland* was definitely not conceived as a merchant raider. She was the result of modern technology, built for a vision of the future of naval warfare. However, having created a new type of ship, the Naval High Command realised that it was the ideal tool for commerce raiding and developed plans to send surface ships into far-off regions for the sole purpose of harassing merchant shipping. The idea was not so much to sink ships, but to draw enemy warships away from more pressing objectives and to cause convoys to be re-routed along lengthy diversionary routes. The ensign of the Reichsmarine flying on the stern indicates this picture was taken before the introduction of the swastika in 1935. She was renamed *Lützow* in early in World War 2 and took part in the invasion of Norway in April 1940. She was forced to turn back while supporting the naval invasion force at Oslo when she suffered damage after she was hit by Norwegian coastal batteries.

in, experts became convinced Britain was in the process of applying considerable pressure on Denmark and Norway to make them more 'Allied friendly' and to prevent German convoys from running through their coastal waters. Whatever it was, these deciphered signals emphasised the importance of getting there first to prevent Britain from gaining a foothold on the Continent. Plans for the German invasion of Denmark and Norway were well under way, so beating Britain and France to that objective was a strong possibility.

The Norwegian campaign includes a good example of how one side could have vital information, but not be able to draw any inferences from it. This happened when the Royal Air Force Photo Reconnaissance Unit brought back its first splendidly sharp pictures of Kiel in April 1940. Analysts saw the harbour full of shipping, with masses of transports being loaded, but not having any previous photos with which to compare this activity meant none of them could make any deductions from what they saw. Shortly afterwards the mass of German shipping set sail for the invasion of Norway. Once the bitter fighting in the northern waters around Norway was under way, the Chiefs of the British Naval War Staff did not need analysts to tell them that the coincidences consistently seemed to favour the Germans. Much of the action was quick and decisive, with hard blows being delivered by both sides, but generally it appeared as if the Germans were well prepared with a knowledge of

what British forces were doing. The Admiralty deduced that the Germans had the means of reading the British Naval Cipher in use at the time and ordered the codes to be changed. However, such a complicated task was difficult to accomplish, especially as a good number of relatively inexperienced men were now manning radio rooms of hastily converted ships. As has already been mentioned, it was August before this major change took place, when the Naval Cipher was replaced by Naval Cipher No 2. The Kriegsmarine had suffered a number of losses in the Norwegian campaign to both surface ships and U-boats. Despite the heavy cruiser *Blücher* and light cruisers *Karlsruhe* and *Königsberg* being sunk by Norwegian coastal batteries, assisted by the Fleet Air Arm in the case of the *Königsberg*, serious damage being suffered by the heavy cruisers *Scharnhorst* and *Gneisenau*, the pocket battleship *Lützow* being damaged by the batteries and the heavy cruiser *Admiral Hipper* being damaged when rammed by the Royal Navy destroyer *Glowworm* (the British ship sinking with the loss of much of its crew), the Germans had managed to successfully land enough troops at Narvik, Trondheim, Bergen, Kristiansand and Arendal, and Oslo and then to hold back Allied counter attacks. Two attacks by the Royal Navy at Narvik, where the Germans lost nine destroyers and seven transports, failed to turn the tide and Norwegian resistance ceased in June.

Right:
The light cruiser *Karlsruhe* on a world tour, long before the war, showing a mass of radio aerials strung around the artillery control centre at the top of the tubular tower. One of the funnels can be seen on the right. This photograph was taken at a time when radio engineers could string up all manner of complicated aerials without the small number of anti-aircraft gunners objecting to the restrictions in their field of fire. During the German invasion of Norway in April 1940 she was torpedoed and sunk by a Royal Navy submarine after assisting the German landing at Kristiansand.

Chapter 5
Coastal Waters

Operations in British coastal waters brought with them their own distinctive flavour. A high proportion of ships that Britain employed were auxiliaries and a good number of them were small former fishing boats, but whatever their type, the crews were drawn predominantly from men who sailed these vessels before the war, rather than regulars of the Royal Navy. They were often highly independent individualists who found their way through inhospitable waters almost by instinct and were no respecters of authority. This unique set of characteristics brought with it both advantages and difficulties for their opponents in the Radio Monitoring Service. The easy side was that such men tended to transmit the type of information which it was best for an enemy not to know, but since many of the British auxiliaries did not have fully trained radio operators official procedures were not always followed, which could make it more difficult for an outsider to work out what was going on.

When the war started, a shock reaction appeared to empty the seas of inshore traffic, but once the initial scare was over, shipping re-emerged to continue cautiously plying its coastal trade. Many fishermen, especially those from isolated communities, saw no reason for not going to sea, although their movements were very much at a reduced tempo and scale. As a result, the seas were not swept entirely clear of activity and some radio traffic continued to fill the airwaves. One of the first aims of the Radio Monitoring Service was to distinguish this commercial traffic from military

Above: Many smaller boats in coastal waters carried an impressive array of radio aerials. These formed a vital link with land-based operations rooms but the majority of smaller vessels did not have facilities for intercepting the opposition's broadcasts. In any case, a vast proportion of the small boats carried such small crews that there were not enough men or the space to decode intercepts and evaluate their meaning.

Above: German troops moving into Lorient, with a lorry from the Todt Organisation in the foreground. Although such traffic jams were most trying for the people stuck in them, they were appreciated by the B-Dienst because such commotion tended to make people turn towards their radios to report what was going on.

operations, especially mine laying. It was important to find out where the enemy was creating defensive minefields and, at the same time, discover when there were expeditions to seal off routes near the German coast. As it turned out, there was very little such interference, which was convenient because the B-Dienst was short-staffed and had other, more pressing, events to deal with.

The real crunch, as far as north European coastal waters were concerned, came early in May 1940 when Germany invaded Holland, Belgium and France. The famous Dunkirk evacuations were completed on 5 June and the whole offensive ended on the 22nd, when the French–German armistice was signed. This campaign was an almost exclusive Army and Air Force affair, with the German Navy contributing only a handful of tiny ships for close inshore operations. In any case a large proportion of the Navy's surface ships had been sunk or damaged during the invasion of Norway and Denmark in recent weeks, so many Navy leaders were pleased they did not have to run supplies and troops into coastal towns or support the army with bombardments from the sea.

However, the B-Dienst was still actively engaged in keeping tabs on the proceedings in the Low Countries and provided the High Command with an accurate picture of what was going on. For example, Bonatz later stated that the B-Dienst's first indication that French, Belgian, Dutch and British forces were cut off on the coast came from enemy sources. The German advance had been so rapid and fragmented that one part of the ground forces could not keep in touch with another and the higher command centres were often not one hundred per cent sure exactly where the first echelons had got to. Therefore the additional intelligence from Allied signals was most informative.

In addition to such welcome news, the B-Dienst intercepted details of Royal Air Force bombing targets, Allied convoy movements, details about their escorts, minesweeping activities, as well as valuable intelligence on supply and evacuation routes. It was also discovered that Britain seemed to know about some German parachute drop zones shortly before the aircraft arrived, suggesting there was a serious leak somewhere in Luftwaffe operations. Although such information was of great value, the big challenge for the B-Dienst was to determine what the Royal Navy was doing, and whether there was any prospect of big ships being thrown into the offensive to bombard coastal towns. Resistance in towns such as Rotterdam, Calais and a good number of other places resulted in considerable unnecessary destruction, and the possibility of heavy guns from battleships adding to Germany's problems was indeed a major threat, especially as the German Navy was in no position to oppose such moves.

The B-Dienst identified a big naval squadron, consisting of the cruisers *Arethusa*, *Birmingham*,

Above: The remains of British trucks in Dunkirk, during or shortly after the famous Allied evacuation. Such chaos provided the B-Dienst with masses of interesting background information and sometimes supplied the essential information for understanding the numerous code words in current usage. Although radio operators tended to destroy their equipment and secret code books, they usually left considerable quantities of worthwhile material behind. Maps and charts showing routes were most welcome booty for the naval intelligence.

Calcutta and *Galatea*, in the northern reaches of the North Sea, but could not find any indications whether any of them were due to move south. Neither was there a great deal of big ship activity at the western end of the English Channel, so it looked as if nothing much bigger than a destroyer was likely to be encountered, which was most pleasing for German coastal commanders. The only unexpected commotion came when a British radio suddenly burst into hectic life to announce the presence of a German battleship with destroyer escorts approaching the English Channel. The B-Dienst couldn't work out which battleship it was likely to be and a quick

Above: KptzS Hans Rösing (FdU:West: Flag Officer for U-boats West) and ObltzS Hans Seidel (*U361*) with female employees and the standard large radio, in its pride of place. In 1933, when Hitler came to power, radios were still a highly technical and an expensive dream for a small number of enthusiasts. For many of his early speeches he can be seen talking into a microphone which was almost as big as the radio in this picture, but progress was incredibly rapid and it was not long before the majority of ordinary people could afford to buy their own receivers. Yet, as this picture shows, they were large, cumbersome and very heavy. Listening to them was not always easy. They crackled, hissed and provided a multitude of other background noises. However, they made it possible for the authorities to communicate with a large proportion of the population at once and to pass on urgent messages, which would otherwise have taken days or weeks to reach their destinations.

enquiry to the Supreme Naval Command revealed only that a flotilla of eight E-boats, together with their tiny support tender, were on their way along the Dutch coast. This misidentification produced a few smirks and left men wondering when the opposition was going to notice its mistake. The Royal Navy did not oblige by sending an embarrassing correction.

On the ground the German advance rushed to the Channel coast within days. A conglomeration of almost half a million men pulled together into a last stand near Dunkirk, where they were without adequate harbour facilities and the beaches were protected by shallow water, which prevented the majority of large ships from approaching too close. Today, we are usually given the impression that this evacuation ran smoothly in united harmony, but German decrypts tend to show a different picture: one of criticism, argument and utter frustration.

A good many of the small boats participating in the evacuation were forced into this predicament, without the crews themselves being terribly keen on crossing into a dangerous war zone. Even today, there are still occasional rumblings along the Channel coast about men who failed to do their duty. Apparently a number of boats sailed halfway across and then turned round again to return empty. Decrypts made by the B-Dienst confirm this lack of enthusiasm. On 1 June, for example, the Vice-Admiral Bertram Ramsay (commanding the evacuation from Dover) sent a terse message to naval units at sea ordering them to force empty boats back to France and to make sure they picked up men from the beaches.

There were also disputes when the British wished to take over merchant ships belonging to the countries now being overrun by Hitler. The crew of the 8,156 gross register tons (grt) Dutch freighter *Amstelland* objected most strongly and left Portland without permission on 27 May, in a desperate bid to get back home to Amsterdam. Exactly what happened is not clear, but the Commander-in-Chief for the Western Approaches sent a detailed description of the ship, with orders to escort her to the Downs (the sea area to the north of Dover, between Kent and the Goodwin Sands). What happened during the next few days is impossible to reconstruct

Above: During the war a labyrinth of minor connecting passages and larger working tunnel were cut through the relatively soft chalk underneath Dover Castle. These tunnels were major communication and operation centres for the British. The majority of the British naval operation centres in Dover were in fact not situated in the modern sections of the tunnel system under Dover but in much older casemates built partly by French prisoners of war during the Napoleonic era. This picture shows some of the old, brick-lined tunnels inside the White Cliffs of Dover. Vice-Admiral Bertram Ramsay worked, and there was even a bed in his room, in a tunnel similar to those shown here, albeit much larger.

Above: Makeshift naval officer quarters somewhere in occupied France with the all-important radio taking centre stage. People would gather around to listen to broadcasts, in a similar fashion to the way they would now sit watching television. The white screen in the middle of the radio is a piece of cloth covering the massive speaker inside.

from decrypts, but we do know the *Amstelland* was sunk on 1 July 1940 by *U65* (Kptlt Hans-Gerrit von Stockhausen) in the Atlantic, southwest of Ireland, while sailing in convoy OA175.

B-Dienst decrypts of messages from the coastal waters make it quite clear how well Britain benefited from the lack of inter-service co-operation in Germany and by the absence of an effective German naval air arm. Over and over again the Radio Monitoring Service deciphered a flood of messages, but found there were no forces available to take appropriate countermeasures. For example, details of British destroyers towing five disabled Dutch submarines across the North Sea were intercepted in good time, but nothing was available to prevent the escape. It was also learned that the destroyer *Whitley* had been stranded near Dunkirk, but again, all the B-Dienst could do was to provide an up-to-the-minute salvage report, knowing nothing was likely to interfere with the attempts to refloat the ship.

Even when the Dunkirk evacuation had scarcely ended, decrypts suggested that London was becoming increasingly edgy about a possible German move to cross the English Channel. The first definite decrypt relating to an expected German invasion came on 10 June, when the Rear Admiral (Submarines) broadcast a general warning of an invasion along England's east coast, and available forces were employed accordingly. This sounded absurd enough in German intelligence circles to be taken as a hoax, but the intercepted messages were no hollow threats or put-up jobs, and were supported by very real activity at sea. Yet the B-Dienst could not work out where such resources for a German crossing of the Channel and North Sea should come from or how this was likely to be carried out. All this suggested British intelligence of German naval resources was exceedingly poor because there were no major movements afoot at the time to indicate an assembly of the necessary shipping was taking place.

Today, the masses of plans, counter-plans, genuine deception efforts and postwar generated hoaxes have become tightly intertwined, making it hard to separate fact from fiction and to work out exactly what was being premeditated. Although Germany later prepared for an invasion of England's south coast, this now looks more like a half-hearted attempt at intimidating Britain, rather than a serious effort to cross the Channel. Entire books have been written on this subject and therefore there is no point in elucidating this any further in the space available here, especially as the B-Dienst was hardly involved with the planning.

When the hectic few weeks of the intense fighting in Holland, Belgium and France drew to a close, the B-Dienst returned to its normal drudgery of trying to make sense of the day-to-day mundane activities in coastal waters. Much of this was boring, time-consuming and virtually impossible to sort out. Signals such as, 'Had cold potatoes for lunch now passing Felix put kettle on' could merely be fishermen's private messages or a highly important coded transmission. Many such messages came as individual signals, rather than part of longer sequences which therefore made it much harder to make sense of them. The daily routine consisted of ups, when signals were easy to follow, or deep downs when everything was decrypted into plain English but still did not reveal any significant meaning. The only way to deal with these was to leave them in some dark corner until they were conveniently forgotten. Yet, slowly and bit by bit, some of the more obscure messages started to make sense. For example an earlier signal, suggesting convoys could sail through coastal minefields, was solved when it was realised the mines were laid parallel to the coast with enough space between them and the land for shipping to pass unhindered, even at the lowest tides. It also became evident that some areas of the minefield were left open for fishermen.

These details were especially interesting, but the decrypted information about safe routes through mined waters was even more useful. Unfortunately the long summer days made excursions into British waters somewhat impractical. Earlier in the year, and during the previous autumn, the B-Dienst had been more effective in identifying the coastal convoy routes and keeping close tabs on minesweeping flotillas. Then it was easy to identify the sweeps and to intercept the 'mine clear' signals, making it possible for destroyers and U-boats to creep in during the bad visibility of the long, dark winter nights to plug these gaps with a few surprises. At the same time, the B-Dienst also managed to establish that operations by surface ships were never suspected and that Britain attributed all such intrusions to aircraft or U-boats. This earlier mining offensive was successful not only in sinking a good number of ships but also in bringing the entire coastal convoy system to a standstill for days on end.

Above: A coastal lookout station in occupied France: Le Havre 1941. The man on the right is looking through especially high-powered binoculars, which also double up as range finder. This was most useful, since estimating distances over featureless water is difficult even when conditions are perfect. These stations would have communicated with their headquarters by field telephone, which often did not have sufficient power for ringing bells. Therefore they were fitted with a hand winding dynamo to make the bell ring at the other end. Although primitive, this robust equipment worked very well, and many of these systems remained in use until long after the war. This obviously posed picture shows a member of the Kriegsmarine, a naval anti-aircraft gunner, a soldier from the army's coastal artillery and an infantry observer.

Although Germany now had access to the entire French coast, the chances of repeating these staggering mining performances with large ships such as destroyers were slim as Britain became increasingly vigilant, yet the prospects looked promising enough to consider attacks by fast motor torpedo boats. Since it is easy to be confused by names, some clarification might be helpful here: German motor torpedo boats were known in Britain as E-boats, meaning 'enemy boats' but are more correctly called *Schnellboote* ('fast boats'), usually abbreviated as S-boats. In the German Navy a torpedo boat was a much larger type of vessel which looked more like a small destroyer.

The S-boats reaped some impressive successes close to the British shore, although not all of these were achieved with their intended weapon but with mines. Keeping tabs on individual S-boat operations was not easy. They preferred poor visibility and operated at night whenever possible, crossing the narrow coastal waters after sundown and then sneaking slowly in to make their attacks; their superior speed was usually reserved for escaping retribution after their strike by vanishing into the distance.

The overall results were encouraging and Britain very quickly changed its approach to go on the offensive against the S-boats. It was not long before S-boat commanders

Above: Telephones required land cables and laying these, especially in times of war, was not always easy. A large drum was usually mounted on the back of a truck, which then drove slowly from one destination to another, while a team of men secured the wire to whatever was around. This was more than impractical for highly mobile units, especially artillery, and these groups relied more or less exclusively on radio communications, making it possible for an eavesdropper to get an insight into what they were up to. This shows a German mobile light anti-aircraft unit in occupied France.

Above: The communication huts at the headquarters for FdU:West (Flag Officer for U-boats: West) at Angers in France. The buildings were built into existing woodland to make them less conspicuous from the air. The B-Dienst operated from similar huts at this location.

Above: This obviously posed picture was taken in the communications centre of FdU:West at Angers in France.

reported how British forces were no longer lingering as potential targets, but instead small groups of fast moving boats and aircraft intercepted the Germans whenever they tried crossing the seas into the coastal convoy routes. The B-Dienst was astonished by the apparently vast number of eyes floating around to report the presence of S-boats. Much of the coastal traffic had come to a halt and the waters between the Continent and England usually looked serenely deserted, but somehow it was becoming increasingly difficult to cross them without being noticed. Although this may have annoyed S-boat crews, the B Dienst was delighted with the help that such encounters gave in providing an accurate picture of Britain's soft spots and danger areas. Later, when radar started to make an even greater impact, the Germans found many radar stations to be broadcasting direct to ships at sea, with these messages providing a good source of intelligence about the performance of British equipment. S-boat operations were not limited to those Channel areas in close proximity to the French coast, but extended far up the East Anglian coast and beyond to wreak havoc in places like Yarmouth, Cromer and the Humber estuary.

It was in the more northern reaches of the continental side, near the small Dutch harbour of Den Helder, where S-boats achieved one of their most significant victories as far as radio monitoring was concerned. The story broke over the airwaves shortly before 08.00 hours in the morning of 11 September 1940, when the British Motor

Gun Boat *MGB334* sent a signal saying *MGB335* had been taken in tow by an E-boat. The B-Dienst knew that a few small British boats were lurking off Den Helder, but could not determine exactly what they were doing there. Further signals from the British side suggested that *MGB334* had been in close contact with the captured boat until superior German forces scared it away. These signals included the information that code books and other radio secrets aboard *MGB335* had not been destroyed by the time *MGB334* departed. Although there had been no communication with the S-boat and it has not even been identified, the news was exciting enough to dispatch an intelligence team to Den Helder to give the prize a thorough going over. This paid tremendous dividends. A great deal was recovered during a thorough search. There were folders with details of radio procedures and secret code books, as well as the equipment itself, providing the Germans with much useful information. The B-Dienst wanted to work fast, to extract as much value as possible before Britain closed down the entire coding system which had been carried by the motor gun boat, but this proved to be unnecessary. Very much to Germany's surprise, it appeared as if nothing had been changed, providing the opportunity to exploit the haul to full advantage.

Right and below: The longwave transmitter used by the FdU:West. Not only did this equipment require a large building to accommodate it, but it also consumed considerable quantities of electricity. Mains electricity was not terribly reliable in wartime and all the major German transmitters had their own generator systems to prevent breaks in vitally important transmissions.

Opposite top: The Telex Room at FdU:West. By the time World War 2 started, Germany had produced two main types of machines for sending typed messages along telephone cables. The original, basic model connected two typewriter-like machines to one another and anything typed on one was printed on the other. Of course, the speed of transmission depended on the efficiency of the typist, and this could be increased by using an improved version where the messages were first typed on to punched paper tape. This was then fed into the telex transmitter for automatic dispatch. One of these punched paper machines, holding a reel of tape, can be seen towards the right of the picture. Such machines were exceedingly noisy and therefore sound-protecting partitions were necessary if people wanted to hear themselves speak. The large box to the right of the door is a small, portable radio.

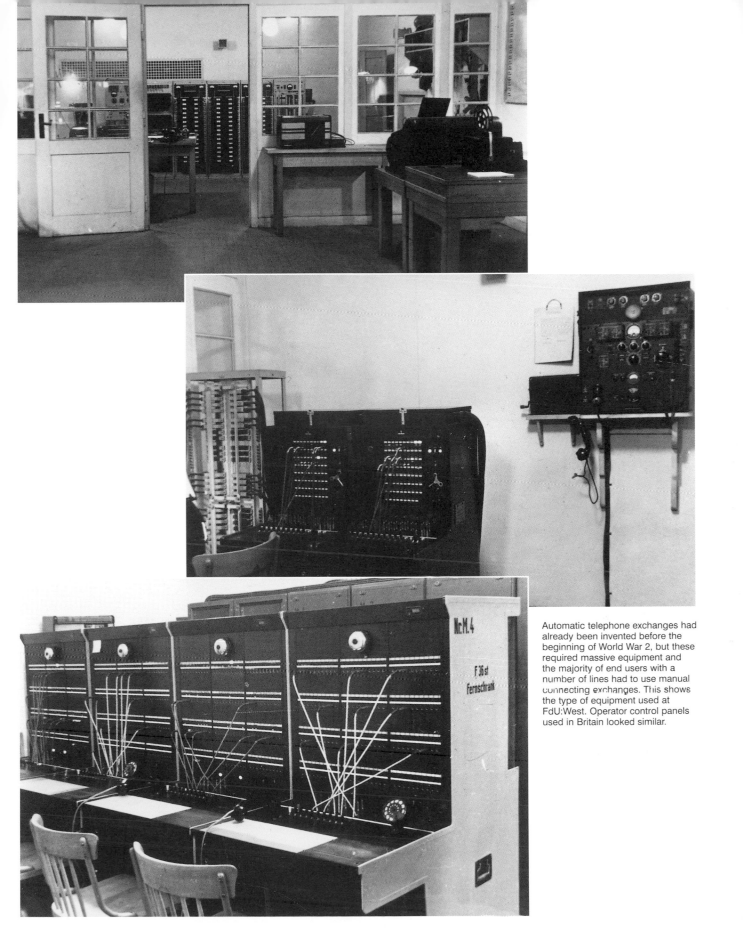

Automatic telephone exchanges had already been invented before the beginning of World War 2, but these required massive equipment and the majority of end users with a number of lines had to use manual connecting exchanges. This shows the type of equipment used at FdU:West. Operator control panels used in Britain looked similar.

Right:
The inside of the telex room at the radio complex of the FdU:West (Flag Officer for U-boats: West) near Angers in France, which also accommodated a branch of the B-Dienst. The man appears to be operating a manual telex machine, while an automatic, punched paper strip machine can be seen towards the left. Although well protected by a large body of guards, operators kept their rifles at the ready and gas masks were also close at hand.

Left:
An office inside a hut at Angers in France, showing the type of accommodation used by the B-Dienst.

Right:
The top-secret telex room within the radio complex near Angers in France. The box on the table in the foreground is a military telephone with a winding handle to make the bell ring at the other end. These tended not to be connected to the main telephone network, but were used for direct line connections between only a few centres.

Chapter 6
Surface Raiders

Although the big guns of *Admiral Graf Spee* (KptzS Hans Langsdorff) and *Deutschland* (KptzS Paul Wenneker) as well as their supply tankers had taken up waiting positions in lonely parts of the Atlantic before the outbreak of war, permission to commence hostilities was withheld for more than three weeks until 25 September 1939. Hitler was hoping for a quick conclusion to the Polish campaign and therefore did not want to aggravate the government in London by sinking its ships in far distant waters. Since both these pocket battleships were expected to remain at sea for several months without a great deal of support, they were provided with a rich assortment of survival aids including extensive radio monitoring facilities. In addition to this, they were not only excluded from the general wartime prohibition on tuning in to foreign broadcasts, but there were even linguists on board who had this as one of their main duties. Planners realised that listening to such news could

well turn into a two-edged sword and these men might be taken in by convincing foreign propaganda. In view of this, their written instructions contained some strongly worded passages dealing with the righteousness of their cause and the need to believe in their own ultimate victory. It was made clear that foreign broadcasts were likely to show Germany in a bad light by presenting half-truths and lies.

After leaving Germany, *Graf Spee* and *Deutschland* vanished into the vastness of the restless ocean for the first four weeks of the war and it was 30 September 1939 when the B-Dienst intercepted the first news. This came in the form of a distress call from *Graf Spee's* first victim, the British freighter *Clement*. The following day the Admiralty in London issued a general raider warning for the Pernambuco area and this was relayed from Germany in special code, in case it had not been picked up by the pocket battleships. It seems likely Langsdorff

Above: Meetings on the high seas were relatively rare, but vitally important for passing on the latest news. Warships, including the disguised ghost cruisers, usually had specialist men for evaluating the information trickling in, but merchant ships running the blockade often had to do without such luxuries and the men in them had to rely on their own wits to outsmart the enemy.

Above: The *City of Durban*, from Ellerman Lines of Liverpool, a 5,850grt turbine freighter with some passenger accommodation. Note the massive radio aerial stretching from the foremast to the funnel and with a wire running down from the funnel to the radio shack behind the bridge.

would also have been reminded to move his operations area further south. Following this, the ether went quiet again and nothing more was heard for three weeks. Three more ships were sunk during this period, but two of them did not use their radio and the distress call from the other, the freighter *Huntsman*, was not acknowledged by Britain and therefore probably not picked up. Neither was it repeated by anyone else. Such repeats were common practice. Both coastal radios and operators aboard ships relayed distress calls if they were not acknowledged.

Strangely enough, the call from *Huntsman* was intercepted in Germany, to provide the Supreme Naval Command with a possible position for the pocket battleship. Missing such brief signals was common and does not mean that the Admiralty was sitting idly by. B-Dienst found considerable indications in the airwaves of a number of powerful hunting forces being assembled to make sure the raider would not get back home. Today it is well known how the pocket battleship ran into the British cruisers *Exeter*, *Ajax* and *Achilles* in the La Plata Estuary of South America and how the ensuing battle resulted in *Graf Spee* being scuttled. This, in itself, was a major act of deception in which radio played a significant role. Britain managed to convince Langsdorff that he was surrounded by superior forces to make an attempted breakout sheer folly which would result in certain death.

Incidentally, in those days there were many sea areas with very little radio traffic throughout much of the day and certain times were set aside for transmitting special messages. This was well known to the German merchant navy and details were passed on to raiders so that they would know the most vulnerable times and could attack when the radio rooms in merchant ships were less likely to be manned.

Although nowhere near as dramatic as *Graf Spee's* scuttling, *Deutschland* also had an eventful cruise nearer home, in the North Atlantic, but instead of dramatic battles the story centred on the ship's temperamental machinery and the stirring up of an unexpected political row. This started on 9 October 1939 when an American freighter with passenger accommodation, the *City of Flint*, was captured to be sent to Germany with a prize crew. When the ship turned up in a north Russian port, to collect orders for sailing south, the Americans were outraged. However, despite extensive activity, the Royal Navy's efforts to bring the *Deutschland* to battle failed miserably and she had been back in Gotenhafen (Gdynia), in the far eastern Baltic, for several weeks before the Admiralty in London discovered her whereabouts.

One aspect of this early raider campaign was that German planners failed to adequately protect their own merchant fleet. A few days before the beginning of war, the Naval High Command told its merchant ships to run for home or to make for a neutral port, if they could not get back within three days. Yet, despite this, there were still several dozen or more ships left floundering at sea, without any support to get into a safe haven. Early radio intercepts made it quite clear how Britain and France were establishing special forces for the sole purpose of bringing the raiders to battle, and shortly afterwards it became obvious these Allied hunters were also highly

successful in finding German ships running the blockade. The search for *Graf Spee* and *Deutschland* resulted in a dozen or more German merchant ships being sunk, scuttled or captured and all the B-Dienst could do to help was to provide the Supreme Naval Command with a list of distress calls as they poured in.

International law allowed merchant ships from warring nations to remain in neutral ports, but they were not allowed to aid their side nor use their radio. What actually happened in these cases depended on the local authorities. Some ships had their radio transmitters removed, others had them sealed, while there were cases where a promise not to use the equipment was sufficient. Such laxity was sometimes used to pass information to the B-Dienst.

The B-Dienst was still terribly understaffed during this first autumn of war and had very little information about the other side to help ships at sea or in foreign ports. It was often possible to intercept messages, but the sheer volume of traffic made it impossible to decipher every one. In addition to this, the B-Dienst was still lacking the expertise to work out the exact wording of some signals, which meant it had no choice other than to take the role of a passive observer for this first raider

Above: The German merchant ship *Anneliese Essberger*, with the circular radio direction finder aerial visible. August 1941 was an especially fraught period for *Anneliese Essberger's* blockade-breaking run from the Far East to Bordeaux in France. Three British auxiliary cruisers, *Queen of Bermuda*, *Alcantara* and *Asturias*, were known to be in the area and the lookouts had to remain fully alert to avoid running into such powerful opposition.

offensive. This situation changed rapidly and when Germany repeated the venture, it was possible for the Radio Monitoring Service to make a far more significant contribution.

A similar operation to the *Admiral Graf Spee* and *Deutschland* cruises was launched a year later, when the pocket battleship *Admiral Scheer* (KptzS Theodor Krancke) slid through the Denmark Strait, between Iceland and Greenland, during the last night of October 1940. *Scheer* had been in dock for a major refit when the war started and this was her first long war cruise. Neither Germany nor Britain had any idea of the ship's whereabouts until 5 November, when the armed merchant cruiser *Jervis Bay* under Captain E. S. F. Fegen, reported the presence of a German raider and ordered convoy HX84 (Halifax in Nova Scotia to the UK) to scatter. The story of how the plucky *Jervis Bay* stood up to the superior firepower of the pocket battleship and how Captain Fegen was awarded a posthumous Victoria Cross after his ship was sunk along with five of the convoy, has been told often enough. At the height of this battle, the German B-Dienst was not greatly concerned with the news that the convoy was vanishing under cover of smoke and that only five merchant ships were sunk from a total of 37, but what the Admiralty was doing elsewhere in the area. It was imperative that other warships should not get close enough to damage *Admiral Scheer* and this aspect of the backup operation was a success. Once the attack on the convoy was over, *Scheer* needed to be told fairly definitely how best to avoid possible punishment from superior forces.

The main objective for the German code breakers lay in finding out what was going on around *Admiral Scheer*. *Hood* and *Repulse*, together with three ships from the 15th Cruiser Squadron, put out of Scapa Flow to blockade the French Atlantic ports, while *Rodney* and *Nelson* were dispatched to block off the northern route back to Germany. Although Britain was still not sure who was actually out in the North Atlantic, the Admiralty thought it might well be a pocket battleship and therefore held out little hope of catching it in its net. As had been anticipated, *Admiral Scheer*, with its enormous range, headed towards the sun, to vanish in the warmth of the South Atlantic. The news that this route was likely to be safe was transmitted from Germany but, no doubt, the B-Dienst officers aboard the pocket battleship also worked this out for themselves. *Admiral Scheer* was to continue raiding successfully over a vast area and survived until the end of the war.

Almost one month later, when the general hubbub had died down, the heavy cruiser *Admiral Hipper* performed the same trick of appearing in the shipping routes of the North Atlantic, after having passed unseen through the Denmark Strait during the night of 6–7 December 1940, while vision was blocked by heavy snowstorms. Once again, neither Britain nor Germany knew where the heavy cruiser was lurking until an eruption of signals suggested something unusual was going on. This was most confusing at first, giving the B-Dienst the biggest of problems in trying to make sense of the transmissions. It seemed as if every ship in a convoy had started transmitting at once, filling the airwaves with unintelligible code. *Hipper's* attack on convoy WS5A (UK to Suez and Bombay) was clear, but it took a while for the ether to quieten down and for one signal at a time to be transmitted. Deciphering these was easy and quick, and presented the Germans with all sorts of information. For example, *Hipper* was also using her radio to report the ships under attack, saying each one was sinking. These ships themselves then corrected the heavy cruiser with the news they were only damaged, and not sinking. Then the heavy cruiser *Berwick* and other ships from the convoy's escort intervened, causing *Hipper* to abandon the attack and to make off at high speed.

Now the hunt was on and the B-Dienst personnel aboard *Hipper* and in offices back home were going to play a vital part in extracting her from what could turn into a most precarious predicament. *Hipper* could not repeat *Scheer's* disappearing act by vanishing into the South Atlantic because the high-pressure steam turbines of heavy cruisers were nowhere near as economical or reliable as the diesel engines of pocket battleships. The B-Dienst worked out that going back to Germany was impossible. Intercepts indicated there were too many guns blocking the way, but the path to France was relatively clear, and since the cruiser was experiencing considerable trouble with its temperamental engines, it was decided to make for Brest, which the *Hipper* reached on 27 December 1940. German surface raiding activities continued in early 1941. *Scharnhorst* and *Gneisenau* were sent into the North Atlantic in January 1941 where they operated with considerable success against convoys and lone merchantmen for two months, although under instructions not to engage with comparable forces. They returned to Brest in late March. *Hipper* also embarked on another raiding cruise in February in the South Atlantic, returning briefly to Brest before making for Norway.

By early 1941 the newly commissioned German battleship *Bismarck* was successfully completing her training and getting ready for a sortie into the convoy routes of the North Atlantic. Although one would have expected the concept of the unsinkable ship to have gone down with the *Titanic*, somehow it surfaced again to provide the German naval hierarchy with unshakeable faith that the battleship *Bismarck* was going to be the answer to many problems. Strangely enough, it was a landlubber, the Austrian Adolf Hitler, who turned to the admirals on the launching day to ask what was going to happen if a torpedo struck the massive rudders. A short time later exactly this Achilles' heel played a central part in one of the most dramatic sea battles of all time.

Germany's plan was for *Bismarck* to rampage around

Left:
A German Heinkel
He115 flying low over
the blockade breaker
Anneliese Essberger with
a couple of the wires for
the radio aerial In the
foreground. The ship
was expected and the
aircraft was sent out
from France to find her.
Using radio at this
critical stage of the
voyage was considered
too dangerous because
the broadcast could give
away the position to the
Allies.

Above: Pocket battleship *Admiral Scheer* is seen after her refit at the beginning of the war, showing what she looked like when she appeared in the shipping lanes as a merchant raider. She then carried equipment for intercepting the opposition's radio transmissions and also had special B-Dienst staff on board to evaluate any information gathered. Although the voyages of the surface raiders have been well documented by men who took part, and the role of the intelligence officers has been praised, there is little recorded evidence as to exactly how this intelligence gathering was organised or how it worked. In many cases we are now left with the knowledge that intelligence evaluation played a crucial role in the survival of the ghost cruisers, but it is difficult to reconstruct how the vital clues were unravelled by the Germans.

in the Atlantic sea lanes but Britain could not afford such a marauding giant on its vulnerable supply routes and therefore had to strike hard before it vanished into the vastness of the ocean. The big problem for Britain was knowing exactly when *Bismarck* was going to set out. If the might of the Home Fleet sailed too early, it could easily run out of fuel at the critical time. If it left too late, *Bismarck* could slip through the fogs of the Denmark Strait into the open ocean, not to be found again. Germany, on the other hand, knew full well that the success of such an operation depended on being able to break out without being detected and therefore imposed strict radio silence on both *Bismarck* (KptzS Ernst Lindemann) and her consort, the heavy cruiser *Prinz Eugen* (KptzS Helmuth Brinkmann) when they sailed out of Gotenhafen (Gdynia) on the night of 18/19 May 1941.

Britain was warned of the ships moving west through the Baltic and reconnaissance aircraft discovered them in Korsfjord (Norway) on 21 May. Although no news was expected from the two German ships, the B-Dienst was on full alert, trying to ascertain what the British Navy and Air Force were doing and where threats were likely to be coming from. Special officers aboard both ships were provided with the latest news of British fleet dispositions before they sailed and this was updated by radio as soon as changes were identified. The brief refuelling of *Prinz Eugen* in Norway took place during appallingly bad weather when many normal air reconnaissance flights were grounded, but two lone pilots, Flying Officers C. A. S. Greenhill and Michael Suckling, took off in an attempt to locate the two big ships, and Suckling finally identified her while she was on the verge of leaving Norway. It seems highly likely he did not use his radio and reported the matter only when he returned to base. Yet, somehow, despite the silence in the ether, Germany got to know about *Bismarck* having been sighted. The British orders to the Home Fleet were passed on by land lines and by visual signals, but a few clues leaked out. In addition to this, Berlin also knew from intercepts about an increase in cruiser patrols for the Faroe area and in the Denmark Strait. (Since writing this text it has come to light through Enigma decrypts that a brief radio signal from *Bismarck* was intercepted by British code breakers. The Admiralty therefore knew definitely the two ships were in Norway, but still sent reconnaissance planes so as not to give away any clues of Britain reading the German cipher.)

Bismarck and *Prinz Eugen* had hardly left when the Commander-in-Chief Western Approaches sent an Operational Urgent signal. These were quite easy to identify, but deciphering them took a lot longer. At first this was taken to be a sighting report, but it turned out to be a general warning that heavy enemy forces were at sea. At about the same time, there was a set of lengthy signals to Gibraltar with news of *Bismarck's* breakout.

This told the B-Dienst which forces were on the move from the southern area, but not what was in the process of leaving British or Canadian ports. Following this, the ether settled into an uneasy silence once more, with a large number of intercept stations on full alert, waiting for something to develop. The first indications of hunters having found the scent was when a British cruiser, later identified as *Suffolk*, sent a sighting report on 23 May. This was heard by another cruiser, *Norfolk*, and by Berlin, but apparently not by anyone in Britain. Germany assumed the B-Dienst staff aboard *Bismarck* and *Prinz Eugen* would probably have picked it up as well. *Norfolk* sent another sighting report when she came on the scene and this was later followed by a chain of similar signals. These were made up of pretty standard wording and were relatively easy to decipher. An interesting point about them was that the positions given by the two ships differed by well over 100 kilometres, making it impossible to work out exactly where they were.

The dramatic sinking of the battlecruiser *Hood* by the *Bismarck* that quickly followed on 24 May also went without commentary in the airwaves. The first Germany knew about something dramatic having happened was when the regular flow of messages from radio station 0TT (the *Hood's* call sign) suddenly went off the air. Then, shortly afterwards, the news of the sinking was broadcast to London and this was quickly followed by a multitude of German and British messages. Of course, the B-Dienst was not concerned with deciphering messages from *Bismarck* and *Prinz Eugen* but kept watch on the German frequencies to use the direction finding system as a check on the ships' location. This quickly provided confirmation that not all was well. Instead of heading for the shipping routes of the North Atlantic, *Bismarck* was making for France (she had been damaged in the attack).

It is difficult to determine from surviving intercepts exactly what the German High Command knew at the time and what was only learned shortly after the event. Berlin did discover at one point that 15 carrier-based torpedo aircraft were ready for take-off — but only as soon as the target had been relocated. This made it obvious that the British had lost track of the *Bismarck*, but sadly for the Germans this was not realised on board and the Fleet Commander, Admiral Günther Lütjens, sent a signal to the Supreme Naval Command on 25 May, thinking they were still being followed. After blundering the process at first, Britain homed in on this, but this was not known to the Germans at the time. Next, on 26 May, a British report told of an airborne torpedo attack against *Bismarck*, but there followed no confirmation from the German side. The B-Dienst had expected a flood of signals once an attack was under way. This was then clarified a few moments later by a protest from the cruiser *Sheffield*, frantically saying she was under attack from carrier aircraft. Luckily for the

Royal Navy, no significant damage was done.

This astonishing interlude was followed by more silence until the German Fleet Commander reported an attack by torpedo-carrying aircraft later the same day. Exactly nine minutes later came another signal saying the ship could no longer be manoeuvred and it was impossible to steer with engines alone. This was followed with news of another torpedo hit amidships but almost immediately the squadron commander of the attacking force sent a signal saying it seemed unlikely that any of his aircraft had scored a hit. Did this mean there had been another attack against a British ship? The B-Dienst was still puzzling over the possibility when *Bismarck* sent a request for a rendezvous with a U-boat to hand over a copy of the war diary, a clear sign of grave problems. Today it is relatively easy to work out the meaning of the signals, but at the time Berlin was somewhat confused and it was not until the Royal Navy reported *Bismarck* to be heading east-northeast, then north-northwest and then north that the steering problem was finally recognised and it quickly became apparent this could not be rectified. Yet, despite this great disadvantage, the general picture still did not look completely gloomy. *Bismarck* reported that the second torpedo hit had not caused any noteworthy damage, and a number of the chasing British battleships reported having to break off for refuelling, so there was still some hope. In Germany it briefly looked as if only the cruiser *Dorsetshire* remained in the operations area the next morning, 27 May, but this had hardly been digested when the sinking of *Bismarck* was triumphantly announced. The B-Dienst continued to monitor the airwaves to discover *Dorsetshire* was picking up survivors until one of the lookouts reported seeing a periscope, which caused the cruiser to withdraw rather quickly, leaving hundreds of men in the water to drown.

Whilst the loss of *Bismarck* grabbed the headlines, morale in the German Navy was also hit when nine out of the 10 supply ships sent to support *Bismarck* were quickly sunk. It was assumed that these had accidentally been caught in the net thrown to catch the battleship and it was not until long after the war that the news came out that Britain was reading the German radio code. Then it was realised this had been a well-planned independent operation.

Throughout this episode, despite the wealth of intercepts, it was still difficult for Berlin to reconstruct the last moments of the *Bismarck*, and the work of sorting and evaluating the decrypts continued for some time. Tying up the wording in the signals with results from radio direction finders resulted in even more confusion as many of the positions given in signals did not match with locations calculated from their own measurements. At the time Germany knew that the one of the battleships *Rodney* or *Renown* (it was *Rodney*) had sent a signal saying *Bismarck* was still afloat and could not be sunk by gunfire, and that the British battleship called briefly at Scapa Flow before making for a dockyard in Boston (US) for repairs. The signal of 13 survivors from *Bismarck* having died of their wounds was also intercepted, but B-Dienst knew little of the situation with *Prinz Eugen* until she eventually reached Brest safely on 1 June.

Above: British officers as prisoners of war are photographed arriving in the Gironde estuary (France) on 19 April 1941 on board the supply ship *Tannenfels*. Their personal belongings, including their sextants, were given back to them. Prisoners of war were a vital source of information and many unwittingly provided the other side's intelligence with a vast array of useful snippets to make future operations more successful.

After the loss of the *Bismarck* the British continued to be nervous about raider attacks. German intelligence was alerted to this by a stream of Morse messages responding to a sighting of the pocket battleship-cum-heavy cruiser *Lützow* (previously named *Deutschland*) (KptzS Leo Kreisch) off the southern tip of Norway. This apparently made the Admiralty so nervous that the battleship *King George V* and the aircraft carrier *Victorious* were sent to sea to prevent another incursion into the North Atlantic. This had hardly been deciphered when it was discovered that several neutral United States warships were also at sea in the Denmark Strait area with the objective of cutting off any surface raiders. In fact, although the Royal Navy feared *Lützow* and *Admiral Scheer* making for the North Atlantic shipping lanes, the German Navy had lost confidence in these raiding activities and were concentrating on smaller-scale activities, sending instead a squadron of heavy ships north to attack the coal mines on Spitzbergen.

By the time *Admiral Scheer* and *Hipper* had appeared in the shipping lanes in early 1941, a number of disguised merchant raiders or ghost cruisers had been at sea for several months. These were also known as auxiliary cruisers or armed merchant raiders. These ships were normal freighters fitted with concealed guns and disguised to look like innocent neutrals. Their heavy guns had been removed from the old pre-World War 1 ships and were no longer terribly accurate, but were far more powerful than the defensive armament fitted to British merchant ships. These ghost cruisers were equipped with the necessary gear to change their superstructures, add false funnels, enough paint to make them fit into the colour schemes of several neutral shipping lines and they had other trappings to make their disguises effective. As part of this, the radio operators were told to react like semi-sloppy merchant men, who did not have a great deal of regard for officialdom. The ships should follow the correct procedure for sending foreign signals, but the Morse code had to stumble along in staccato fashion with odd mistakes, to make it contrast with the fast flow of the military.

Supplying the appropriate wording was not too difficult for the B-Dienst since the airwaves were full of such calls, but keeping this information up to date was most imperative if a German warship was going to fool the Royal Navy. The slightest slip could make the enemy suspicious and possibly mean the difference between life and death. For example, the normal Mayday or SOS had been replaced by the British by SSS for submarine, RRR for surface raider and AAA for aircraft. The appropriate letter was repeated three times at first, but when Germany started sending such signals as well, the system was changed to repeating the letter four times. Such details sealed the fate of the ghost cruiser *Atlantis* (KptzS Bernhard Rogge). When it was challenged by *Devonshire* on 22 November 1941,

Atlantis sent a correct but outmoded reply 'RRR' in the name of the Dutch freighter SS *Polyphemus*. B-Dienst intercepted this and guessed *Atlantis* was not yet aware of the new four-letter system. *Devonshire*, suspicious, then followed a new British procedure and called up the C-in-C South Atlantic in Freetown to ask whether there was any possibility of just having run into SS *Polyphemus*. The answer was negative. *Devonshire* then opened fire from long range to keep clear of possible retaliation and also because her aircraft had in the meantime sighted *U126* (Kptlt Ernst Bauer) seemingly being refuelled by the suspicious ship. *Atlantis* hastened its own end by scuttling, but went down flying the Dutch flag hoping the Royal Navy would think a harmless blockade runner had been sunk and go on looking for the armed raider. The commander of the U-boat, incidentally, was the only person who was trained in submerged attacks and he happened to have been aboard *Atlantis* at this crucial moment. Therefore he was not in a position to launch a counter-attack. In any case, even if had been, the British cruiser was too far away for torpedoes.

Shortly after the outbreak of the war, the Royal Navy broadcast a series of terse messages, telling the Merchant Navy it was impossible to catch raiders unless the ships hunting them knew where to look, and that such information could come only from the victims themselves. Therefore the importance of sending warnings when approached by unknown ships was emphasised over and over again. Unfortunately some of these messages inevitably turned out to be false alarms. The Admiralty got over this hurdle by downgrading the special wartime distress calls, saying no action was going to be taken for about an hour or so. The idea was to provide sufficient time for the calls to be cancelled if they turned out to be unnecessary. The Radio Monitoring Service was quick to catch on to this new procedure and there were several occasions when raiders dispatched their own radio operators to their victims' radio rooms to cancel the previous messages. This worked well until the ships were overdue at their destinations and the Admiralty guessed that they had been intercepted. This German tactic was then blocked by a new system where exactly the same words as the cancelled plain language call were to be sent a second time in code. And finding how this cipher was put together from intercepts was no easy matter. The only way around the problem was for the attacking German ship to send an innocuous-sounding message of deception at the same time as the victim, with the hope of making the distress call unintelligible. However, this hardly helped because for most of the time there were so few RRR signals that the Admiralty often guessed what was going on and early in August 1940 sent a general broadcast asking all ships which heard such messages to take bearings of where they were coming from. This was not quite the end of

Above: The call sign DIBJ , just visible towards the left, above the typewriter, suggests this is the radio room of the supply ship *Ermland*. Interestingly, the cabin is provided with electric light under a triangular black shade but there is also an oil lamp as backup to its left.

the story because the ghost cruiser *Atlantis*, and probably some other raiders as well, found code books aboard captured ships and made good use of the information. There was no way they could transmit the lengthy details to Germany, but they could send a copy back aboard a prize, although this took ages and delivery could not be guaranteed.

One side-effect of the new system of sending distress calls then cancelling them later was that the ether often erupted with all manner of wild messages. For example, as soon as ships realised *Admiral Scheer* was at large, a number of sightings were reported from all corners of the ocean, even from places where the ship could not possibly be. The B-Dienst thought a large proportion of these were probably sparked off by an Allied warship appearing on the horizon and used the information for plotting the positions of enemy hunters. In addition to this, the B-Dienst also intercepted some definite embarrassments. For example, the freighter *Rowallan Castle* sent a distress call, saying it was under attack from a raider. About an hour later came an apology from the armed merchant cruiser *Circassia*, confessing to having shot at the wrong ship.

Keeping radio silence was a basic technique used by raiders, and the majority did not transmit messages until their position had been well advertised through a victim's distress call. In view of this, the Supreme Naval Command in Berlin could only keep tabs on what was going on through signals sent by the enemy. One such useful piece of information was extracted by the B-Dienst from a number of requests for the Norwegian tanker *Jotunfjell*, with the rather unusual call sign of 'LJJJ', to report its position. There was no reply. This was then followed by a general signal to all shipping off South Africa saying it was possible that this ship had been lost on mines near Cape Agulhas and shipping should steer clear of the usual channels. This immediately told the Supreme Naval Command in Berlin that the *Atlantis* had probably achieved one of her aims of depositing mines in the area. At around the same time, the B-Dienst noted an increase in the number of radio messages broadcast from what sounded like warships in the South Atlantic and concluded that hunting forces there were likely to be increasing in number. However, this did not worry the Supreme Naval Command because *Atlantis* was sailing east into the Indian Ocean, where the airwaves were still relatively quiet.

The radio deception war was considered important enough to form an integral part of the raiders' duties. The ghost cruiser *Orion* (Fregattenkapitän Kurt Weyher), which set out in the spring of 1940 shortly after *Atlantis*, was given the task of feigning the presence of a heavy warship in the shipping lanes of the North Atlantic. This was done by broadcasting RRR distress calls and making sure the words 'pocket battleship' could be clearly deciphered. The intention was to distract the British from the concurrent German invasion

Above: KptzS Kurt Weyher at the chart table aboard auxiliary cruiser *Orion*. In those days there were very few modern navigation aids and finding one's way was a case of plotting a line on a paper chart. Such charts were often found intact aboard merchant ships when they were stopped by larger raiders and provided intelligence officers with valuable information about routes being used by British shipping. This became so critical that the Admiralty in London issued an order prohibiting the marking of routes on charts.
Part of *Orion's* operations orders were to broadcast a number of fake distress messages from the South Atlantic to, hopefully, encourage Royal Navy hunting forces to be formed there. In view of this, RRR distress messages were broadcast, saying a merchant ship was under attack by a pocket battleship. (RRR replaced the standard SOS to indicate attack by a raider; SSS indicated attack by a U-boat. The letters were repeated three times at first; this was later changed to being repeated four times.)

of Denmark and Norway. However, the B-Dienst did not detect a single response to *Orion's* signals, making the whole effort fall flat.

Hoax signals and the radio war in general played quite a significant part in the conflict at sea, with the German ghost cruisers cunningly exploiting this technique to its fullest extent. For example, radio operators aboard the auxiliary cruiser *Pinguin* (KptzS Ernst-Felix Krüder) intercepted messages from their British counterparts in the armed merchant cruiser *Alcantara*, saying it was in combat with a disguised raider. It was not difficult to guess that *Alcantara* had run into *Thor* (KptzS Otto Kähler), which was known to be nearby. The great temptation came a day or so later when *Pinguin's* lookouts spotted smoke on the horizon. Krüder's orders were to avoid conflict at all costs, but this time he ordered 'action stations', correctly believing that *Thor* might have been damaged and therefore he might help by drawing hunters away from her. But even more important, he had also found a possible way of tricking the enemy. He thought the Royal Navy would never assume there were two similar ships so close together and it would blame the same raider for both attacks. He therefore allowed the freighter *Domingo de Larrinaga* to send clear distress calls with her position. The interesting point in Krüder's rather cunning scheme was that if the Royal Navy swallowed this deception, then it would certainly calculate the speed of the ship, though none of the German auxiliary cruisers could actually have covered the distance from *Thor* to *Pinguin* in such a short period of time. This trick actually worked and Krüder was later rewarded with the news from prisoners that the Admiralty had estimated the ghost cruisers' average speed to be some 10 knots more than it actually was.

Not all raider commanders helped in such an effective manner. KptzS Heinz Bonatz has told the story of how Konteradmiral Robert Eyssen of the smallest auxiliary cruiser, *Komet*, was responsible for one of the biggest blunders, which he believed caused Britain to change the Merchant Navy Code system at a time when the B-Dienst could easily read it. At first, it was difficult to make a connection between *Komet* and the change in code, but later it became quite clear how an incident in the Pacific triggered this reaction. The problem started shortly after *Komet* and *Orion* (Fregkpt Kurt Weyher) met near the lonely and sparsely inhabited island of Emirau. Eyssen decided this was a good opportunity for setting his prisoners ashore, but Weyher was dead against the suggestion and even took some key men from *Komet* into *Orion*'s cramped quarters. These were later handed over to a German supply-ship-cum-blockade-runner for the voyage back to France. *Komet*'s release of prisoners resulted in them being picked up by Allied ships and informing the Admiralty in London that part of the raiders' success was due to the Germans being able to read the secret Merchant Navy Code. Consequently, London changed the coding tables, leaving Bonatz frustrated because his cryptanalysts could no longer decipher the messages.

The B-Dienst staff aboard the raider *Pinguin* were responsible for catching an entire fleet of three whale factory ships, together with their small whale catchers, deep in the Antarctic. However, there was no point in making the considerable effort of going so far south unless there was a good chance of success. So the radio team monitored transmissions from the whaling fleet for some time before *Pinguin* pounced. This gave them some idea of how many ships there were and the areas where they were likely to be. The effort was so successful that the *Thor* was also told to explore the icy southern waters and possibly repeat *Pinguin*'s success. However, the B-Dienst men on board could not detect any radio traffic in the Weddell Sea and therefore saved the raider the effort of searching those desolate seas.

Above: The 13,301grt passenger ship *Voltaire* belonging to the Lamport and Holt Line in Liverpool was converted into an armed merchant cruiser after the outbreak of war and saw battle with her German counterpart, the ghost cruiser *Thor*. Radio aerials can be seen running up from the bows to the top of the foremast and from there to the funnel. The mass of cables running from the deck to halfway up the mast, to form a conspicuous triangle, were part of the ship's cranes. The booms for these have been fastened at deck level and the wires pulled taught to negotiate rough seas. The colours running up to the top of the mast are international signal flags, but they appear to have been hoisted as decoration, rather than for sending a serious message.

Above: The pocket battleship *Admiral Scheer* and, in the distance, a supply boat are seen photographed from auxiliary cruiser *Thor* in southern waters. Meeting on the high seas was not only an opportunity to fill up with fuel and to exchange films, books and magazines, but was also an occasion where intelligence officers met to discuss latest developments and to plan future tactics.

Above: Part of a boarding party from the auxiliary cruiser *Thor*, photographed in southern waters. These men were chosen from the most able members of the crew. Having to work under often life-threatening conditions meant they needed the quality of remaining calm under pressure and the ability to select the most important secrets likely to be found aboard their quarry. Some of them sent back astonishing and highly secret information, providing raider captains and B-Dienst officers with valuable gems of useful data.

Orion's safe return to the Gironde estuary in France during August 1941 was also largely attributed to the vigilance and efficiency of the Radio Monitoring Service men on board. One major indication of danger was received from an intercepted message sent by the tanker *Ole Jakob*, which had been captured by *Atlantis* and was now acting as a second pair of eyes for *Orion*. A brief message from a Sunderland, intercepted by the tanker, indicated that there were aircraft acting as lookouts for an unidentified cruiser. This news put everybody on full alert and a few days later *Orion's* own reconnaissance aircraft spotted the cruiser some 80 kilometres away. This caused the aircraft to return quickly, without using its radio, and then *Orion* made off at high speed. On spotting smoke a few days later, *Orion* guessed this could be coming from the same British cruiser which had sunk *Pinguin* some 10 days earlier. So, rather than searching out a potential target, *Orion* sped off in the opposite direction.

Pinguin's fate had been sealed by a distress call from her last victim, the tanker *British Emperor*, which included a description of her attacker, after which it was not too difficult for the reconnaissance aircraft from the cruiser *Cornwall* to find the ship responsible. Again, it was attention to detail which sealed *Pinguin's* fate. The aircraft had flown over numerous ships and would perhaps even have left this one in peace had the decks not been almost deserted. The aircrew had got used to seeing waving coloured seamen. Ironically, Krüder had a good number as prisoners, but he ordered them below as soon as the aircraft was first sighted.

By early 1942 Hitler was convinced that the Allies intended to attack Norway or even mount a full-scale invasion. In view of this, he wanted the battlecruisers *Gneisenau*, *Scharnhorst* and the heavy cruiser *Prinz Eugen* to be pulled out of France. Before the Supreme Naval Command could look at the possibility of getting this squadron through the Denmark Strait between Iceland and Greenland, Hitler ordered the ships to sail through the English Channel. The timing of this was critical, especially when looking at the daring feat from the radio monitoring point of view. The B-Dienst was fairly certain Britain was preparing for a breakout by the heavy ships from their French bases and was going to take extensive measures to prevent them from getting home. The B-Dienst could also work out that the majority of this activity centred on the Atlantic to the west of the British Isles and the English Channel remained relatively clear of shipping. Two submarines, *Sealion* and *H34* were identified as being on patrol between Cornwall and northwest France, but this was nothing new. There had always been some activity in this area; therefore the B-Dienst saw nothing out of the ordinary to prevent the German squadron from getting through the Strait of Dover.

Operation 'Cerberus', the by now famous Channel Dash, started at 23.45 hours on 11 February 1942. The three large German ships were escorted by six destroyers and these were later joined by a variety of torpedo boats from Le Havre and other ports along the route. The weather was very much on the German side, with low cloud and only a few small clear patches breaking up the otherwise impenetrable haze. Despite this, the group was apparently spotted by a couple of fighters. The German squadron probably did not see the two fighters out on dawn patrol. After all, there was ample low cloud cover and there appears to be no record of their radio report having been intercepted. The British control centre heard the message, but did not believe the two relatively inexperienced pilots and therefore relayed the wording of 'three battleships heading east' as 'three fishing boats or minesweepers heading east'. Whatever, the most valuable sighting at the most critical time was ignored.

On the German side, a number of intercept stations were especially tuned to wavelengths which might provide early clues about what was happening along England's south coast, especially at what the B-Dienst called Dungeness Radar Station. This base on Romney Marsh, near the small village of Brookland, had both high-level and low-level radar masts, putting it in an ideal location to pick up the German squadron as it came within range of a several large calibre guns near Dover. Telephone calls from Berlin to Boulogne and Calais confirmed the poor visibility was still ideal for the squadron, but no one could believe the British radar stations did not broadcast a warning of the German approach. Were they communicating through land lines? The Dover area was not only bristling with a multitude of guns and observation posts, but there were at least two more identified radar stations, one at Dover and another at St Margaret's at Cliffe. This was a formidable combination, but everything remained quiet.

Unknown to the Germans, a solitary minesweeper, sent out from Dover to search for some baled out airmen, was blocking their path and quickly reported the presence of the three heavy ships with their escorts, but the ensuing hunt was slow in coming and the ether did not erupt into lively activity until after the ships were leaving the Dover Strait. At that point of time, the radar station at the North Foreland reported the presence of big ships at sea. Although Britain was now in a position to hit a hard blow, there were not enough resources, other than a few Swordfish aircraft, to send out in pursuit. Their attack failed as did later destroyer and air strikes. Both *Scharnhorst* and *Gneisenau* were damaged by mines but by early on 13 February had reached safety. That morning, when the heavy cruiser *Prinz Eugen* was nosing cautiously towards the sea locks at the entrance to the Kiel Canal in the Elbe estuary at Brunsbüttel, a war correspondent on board, Walter Schöppe, took a picture of the rising sun and later, when this was printed, he wrote on the back, 'None of us ever expected to see this sight.'

Above: The Royal Navy submarine HMS *Sealion*. The British plans to prevent the break-out by the German ships up the Channel relied on *Sealion*, off the coast of Brest, intercepting the Germans as they left harbour. In the event the German ships slipped out of Brest undetected after nightfall while *Sealion* had withdrawn out to sea to recharge her batteries. *IAL*

Above: A German torpedo boat typical of those which provided close escort support to the large German ships during the Channel Dash and helped to beat off British attacks along the course of the Channel. *IAL*

Above: Although the German battle-cruiser *Gneisenau* suffered some mine damage during the latter stages of the Channel Dash, she managed to reach the safety of the Kiel Canal in the company of *Prinz Eugen*.

Right: The view from the German heavy cruiser *Prinz Eugen* during the Channel Dash, showing some of the accompanying vessels. She managed to reach Kiel without damage after the Channel Dash.

Above: The heavy cruiser *Prinz Eugen* during the famous Channel Dash with what looks like a spider's web of radio aerials strung over the superstructure. There was considerable debate about the exact positions of these wires. The radio people wanted as many as possible, but the gunners tended to object because they interfered with their field of fire, so complicated compromises had to be reached.

Above:
A lookout aboard the heavy cruiser *Prinz Eugen* during the Channel Dash. On his left are three speaking tubes. Although warships contained an incredible tangle of wires, much of the essential information was passed by word of mouth through metal tubes and this most reliable method is in use to this day.

Left:
The heavy cruiser *Prinz Eugen* with a mass of radio aerials in the background. This photo was taken near the time of the Channel Dash. During the Channel Dash radio silence was maintained except for operationally urgent communications. The ships did not even dare to use their big signal lamps in case these powerful beams were intercepted by low-flying aircraft or ships just over the horizon. Visibility was not very good and many British eyes could have been lurking around without being seen by the Germans.

British Coastal Installations During the Channel Dash

The English Channel, looking over towards the White Cliffs of Dover or Hellfire Corner, as the area was called by the British during the war, is only about 30 kilometres from coast to coast at the narrowest point. At low tide one can see the massive banks of the Goodwin Sands blocking the way. These are renowned for wrecking ships and during World War 2 a number of German and Allied ships were grounded on them.

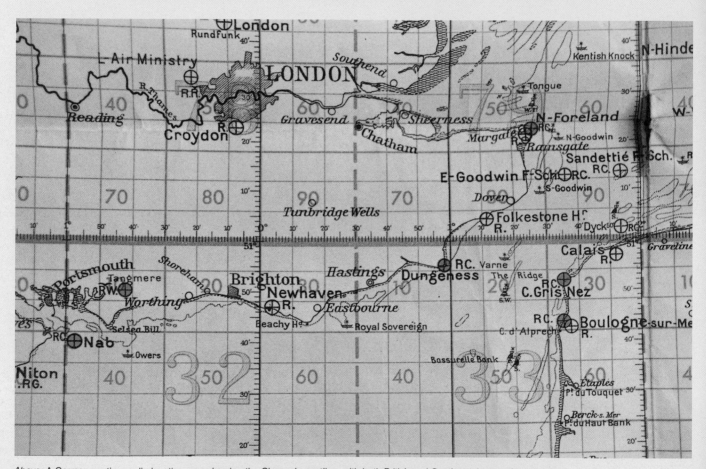

Above: A German wartime radio location map showing the Channel coastline, with both British and Continental transmitters marked.

Above:
The Dover area of southeast England is littered with numerous relics from World War 2, despite a concerted effort to demolish the majority of such installations. This shows the gun battery above Dover harbour, with the foundation securing bolts for medium-sized guns still visible. These gun emplacements were built on top of earlier Victorian structures and historians are helped considerably by each period having used a different type of brick. The World War 2 period is marked by red bricks and concrete, while the earlier phase used a dull yellowish or grey-coloured brick made from London clay.

Left:
The Admiralty Lookout in Dover Castle overlooking the English Channel. Operational radar had only just arrived at the beginning of the war and visual lookouts still played a vital role in monitoring activity in immediate coastal waters. Finding the best vantage points was not difficult, since these spots had been used for centuries, and many of the lookouts of World War 2 were built on top of earlier structures. Underneath this massive concrete box are the remains of a Napoleonic/Victorian-era lookout station.

Right:
The remains of the entrance to one of the radar stations on top of the White Cliffs of Dover. Attempts had been made to cover the entire structure with earth, but during the summer of 1995 it had eroded to such an extent that it was quite easy to walk inside to see a concrete box covering a manhole in the floor. From there a ladder leads down to an extensive underground complex where the labels above the doors of the many rooms were still clearly readable. Although well protected from bombs — the whole complex could also be hermetically sealed in the event of a gas attack as it contained its own ventilation plant inside the underground control centre — these places made themselves vulnerable to eavesdroppers as soon as they started sending information or instructions to ships by radio. However, the radio transmitters were often a considerable distance from the main centre, making it impossible to work out the location of the control room from bearings taken by direction finders.

Above: The remains of what the Germans called Dungeness Radar Station. This was the most feared radio lookout for ships sailing east because it could reveal their position to the guns on top of the White Cliffs of Dover. The station's location is actually a considerable distance inland, near the small village of Brookland — the foundations of the wartime massive 300ft-high masts can still be seen from the main Folkestone–Hastings road. The complex is photographed early in 2002, shortly before redevelopment of the area. The concrete foundations for the 300ft-high (nearly 100m) wooden wartime masts of Dungeness Radar Station, with the main operations building behind. Emergency power plants and the vital workings were located in the lower section of this almost windowless bunker, while the top section was a hollow box filled with shingle, which is so abundant around Dungeness.

Chapter 7
U-boats

When the war started, U-boat operations were restricted by the so-called Prize Ordinance Regulations, which stated that merchant ships could be sunk only if they were carrying contraband and after the safety of the crew and any passengers had been assured. Therefore, theoretically, it was necessary to stop enemy merchant ships, inspect their papers and perhaps even send a search party on board before they could be sent to the bottom. Although these rules made effective submarine operations impossible, Germany went to considerable lengths at first at least to obey the spirit of this law. As a result, the war started with only a few surprise attacks on merchant ships. Britain, however, assumed that Germany would disregard the rules from the start and therefore immediately began arming merchant ships and instructing them to send radio reports of any U-boat attacks. These measures were interpreted as entitling the

Germans to consider the ships as acting in a warlike manner and restrictions on U-boat operations were therefore soon set aside.

Before the war the majority of Royal Navy messages could be read in Germany, it being relatively easy for the Kriegsmarine to understand them. There were some attempts at coding, but it looked as if this was some type of training exercise rather than attempts to deceive eavesdroppers. Some naval transmitters occasionally used the so-called diplomatic cipher, which was based on a comprehensive code book, but the volume was not large enough seriously to engage the German naval intelligence service. Officers there were far more interested in studying the structure of the messages, the procedures used in broadcasting them and the way in which the transmissions were broadcast. Keeping tabs on this was not the easiest of undertakings because a

Above: Smoking fires were not liked by U-boats or German surface raiders because they tended to attract enemy warships, but such scenes of carnage were good news to the B-Dienst back home because they usually resulted in an abnormally high quantity of radio transmissions. Many of such distress calls were made under exceedingly stressful conditions, when radio operators did not think too deeply about maintaining secrecy but were more concerned with getting their message through. In addition, in these situations the captain or master of the ship did not always supply the exact wording to be broadcast which made it more likely that highly secret information would accidentally slip out.

Above: Once back home, commanders and higher officers attended a series of post-mortem discussions, but even when the official interrogation was over, informal groups still assembled to pore over maps and to share experiences. Such in-depth discussions were often more meaningful than the briefings provided by the senior flotilla staff.

good proportion of the material was written in Admiralty Code as a means of shortening messages and the Merchant Trading Code was also used for both personal and administrative transmissions. However, coping with such radio shorthand was quite usual at the time because the majority of the telegraph systems employed some type of procedure for cutting down on the length of wording. In any case, the B-Dienst was under the impression that this was kept relatively simple due to lack of trained operators. Whatever the reasons, keeping tabs on the system was easy enough for the B-Dienst to read the majority of naval signals.

All this came to an abrupt end at the start of the war when the Admiralty Code was replaced with a new military code but as the Royal Navy was a vast, cumbersome organisation there was little or no scope for personalisation and the patterns as well as the wording of messages remained the same as they had been in peacetime. This made it possible to identify the nature of some transmissions and knowledge of the vocabulary used made it relatively easy for the B-Dienst to worm its way slowly into the new system.

The cryptanalysts in Berlin were under the impression that Britain would soon adopt more complicated procedures. There were sufficient indications that the Admiralty knew its code was being cracked. At times, for example, special operations messages were coded slightly differently, making it difficult to gain an immediate insight into the message. In addition, some highly specialised undertakings used a special one-time cipher pad, which was impossible to crack unless one had a copy of the coding sheets and these were captured on only a few occasions. However, this fear of a change in the coding system was not actualised until later in the war.

Gaining an insight into the new coding system after the beginning of the war had been no easy matter, as Germany did not even know how it was put together. Almost 400 people were employed to check intercepted messages with every known coding procedure with the hope of finding out the structure of the new system. This enabled the Germans to gain a fairly rapid insight into the British codes but the amount they could read and the speed at which it was deciphered varied enormously — from times when hardly anything could be understood to periods when messages were deciphered exceedingly quickly.

Britain changed the code again towards the end of 1943, resulting in Germany being locked out once more. This coincided with several direct hits on Naval Headquarters at Tirpitzufer on the side of the Landwehr Canal in Berlin which resulted in a fire gutting the entire building. Although many of the decoding processes had by this time been duplicated in several out stations, the

Above: 14 September 1942. *U405* (Korvkpt Rolf-Heinrich Hopman) was directed by U-boat headquarters towards the crash position of a German aircraft and succeeded in picking up survivors who had baled out. The airmen were lucky to have experienced such calm conditions.

Above: The Atlantic is often much rougher, making it difficult to see very far or indeed to stand up on or in a tiny submarine. This shows the bows of *U181*, under Fregkpt Kurt Freiwald, dipping into the full force of an on-coming gale. The insulators and the single aerial wire are clearly visible. This also served as a safety harness anchorage for men working on the upper deck. Reception with this aerial was very much reduced during conditions like these, but a rod aerial could be raised to improve the radio's performance.

Above and opposite: The Italian U-boat *Tazzoli*, possibly under the command of Carlo Fecia di Cassato, encounters heavy seas. The German High Command was reluctant to slide into a position where its U-boats in the Mediterranean would come under Italian command. Therefore, an autonomous Italian U-boat Command was created in Bordeaux for the few Italian U-boats participating in the Battle of the Atlantic. However, these were supplied with latest German intelligence from the B-Dienst in Berlin via the U-boat Operations Room.

core of the intelligence work was still carried out in this vulnerable building and the B-Dienst never fully recovered from the setback created by the bombing. Germany did gain some understanding of how the new coding system was put together but never managed to read the operational signals in time for action to be taken against them.

By successfully deciphering the Admiralty codes, the B-Dienst knew the sinking figures compiled by both sides were virtually identical, but officers were disturbed to learn how badly the German and British public were misled by being given totally different details. In fact, when the war was about six weeks old, Heinz Bonatz heard a British broadcast claiming to have sunk 22 U-boats, although the Admiralty knew full well the total was only six. Later, he was even more surprised by foreign newspapers reporting blatant lies in speeches made by Winston Churchill in the House of Commons. This told Bonatz that British propaganda was no better than the fancy stories concocted by Josef Goebbels.

Breaking into the newly introduced Merchant Code at the beginning of the war was not too difficult because the vast majority of transmissions followed identical patterns to earlier procedures although the introduction of the new code book did lock Germany out at first. After having gained an insight into the easier Merchant Navy Code, Germany was most surprised to find it was also being used by Royal Navy ships in coastal waters. Vital information, especially from minelayers and minesweepers, was broadcast in the Merchant Navy Code, making it relatively easy for the German Navy to work out the limits of British minefields, safe routes through them and British activities on the continental side of the German Bight.

The Merchant Navy introduced a new system in 1942, but this was quickly cracked and even decoded aboard small ships during special operations. In fact, the German officers responsible for the defence of the Dutch and French coasts had their own men for deciphering broadcasts in their immediate waters, often giving them a running commentary of what was going on just beyond their horizon. However, the good fortune did not last long and the system was made more secure during 1943, becoming complicated enough for the Germans to gain only a partial insight into what was taking place. To make matters more difficult, Britain had developed by this time the means to transmit spoken words over very high frequency radio and understanding the spoken word, with the use of a vast number of code words, was often harder than taking down letters sent in Morse code.

During those first months of war, the B-Dienst was greatly helped by British merchant ships transmitting many messages in plain language and the code used by the rest was easy to decipher. So, good quantities of useful intelligence could be passed on to the U-boats'

operations room, where it was of great value in formulating early plans. One of the most helpful contributions came in the field of radio direction finding, which frightened the majority of U-boat commanders to the point that many refused to use their radio because they were under the impression Britain could determine the position where signals were coming from. Much of this fear was based on prewar propaganda rather than hard facts and it was the B-Dienst which provided the first accurate reports about the performance of British radio direction finders. At least 48 radio direction finders were active during the war, but in those early days the number would have been much smaller. Exactly how many there were and their exact locations were unknown in Germany so extracting even the slightest clue from the airwaves was most valuable. The majority of these outposts sent the data they collected by land line, making it virtually impossible for the B-Dienst to discover their positions, but despite this security a good number of messages were passed on directly by radio. Locating their exact positions was not vital, however. It was far more important to discover their accuracy. Heinz Bonatz cites several cases where the bearings from British stations were intercepted and these produced an error of about 70 kilometres, which resulted in a large sigh of relief in Germany. It certainly looked as if this radio direction finding monster was not as bad as it had been made out. However, at other times the British system produced near perfect results. It appeared as if British radio direction finders lost their accuracy once the source was further than 100 kilometres from land, and beyond a distance of 200 kilometres the figures tended to become totally unreliable. As a result, the Germans assumed Britain was not sure about its degree of accuracy and probably did not pursue many detected U-boats because the Royal Navy could not determine exactly how accurate their figures were. Today we know this was a false assumption. Britain did not have the resources for hunting lone U-boats, unless they were near an operational hot spot.

These German views changed very rapidly when the war was only a few months old and it became clear the British network of radio direction finders was considerably more effective than the initial research had shown. The B-Dienst kept providing the U-boat Command and the Supreme Naval Command with fairly accurate updates of its findings and later even supplied clues about ship-based direction finders, but the higher authorities took hardly any notice of these vital warnings. What is more, later, when B-Dienst specialists pointed to aerials on photographs of warships, saying they could only be radio direction finders, the experts, who supposedly knew about such things, did not consider this evidence important enough and responses to this danger were neglected.

Above: The epitome of the long-distance U-boat commander: Korvkpt Wilhelm Dommes steadies himself against the torpedo-aiming device while riding rough weather in southern waters. When *U178* left Bordeaux on 28 March 1943, Dommes knew he was in for a long arduous voyage, but not that his first officer, Wilhelm Spahr, was going to take the boat home. Having reached the Indian Ocean, Dommes was asked by the U-boat Command whether *U178* could reach the Japanese base at Penang. Although ill and mentally exhausted, and having neither proper charts nor the basic intelligence information for such an undertaking, Dommes agreed to have a go. Yet despite the shortages, there was sufficient expertise on board to deal with all the manner of problems encountered on this voyage to the Orient. Dommes remained in the Far East as Senior German Submarine Officer to pave the way for future long-distance operations from Europe.

For the first weeks of war, the B-Dienst merely kept a general ear open on the airwaves to glean whatever information it could and there were neither great pressures to aim at anything specific nor any emergencies until early on 14 October 1939. Shortly after 02.00 hours the Rear Admiral commanding the British Scapa Flow base issued an Operational Urgent signal. This was most extraordinary from such a source and immediately made everybody sit up. This news had hardly been digested when another warning signal was intercepted. This time it announced the closure of Scapa Flow for all ships bigger than destroyers. Although this information was quickly passed on to officers of the Supreme Naval Command, no one in the B-Dienst had the slightest indication of what was afoot. It was not made clear until 11.45 hours on the 14th when the BBC came on air to announce the sinking of battleship *Royal Oak* inside Scapa Flow, with a heavy loss of life. By that time, the B-Dienst had already deciphered several messages about the urgent organisation of a U-boat hunt in the Orkney area, so it was not difficult to guess what had happened. However, the identify of the boat responsible for penetrating the defences of Scapa Flow was not broadcast on German radio until *U47* (Kptlt Günther Prien) was known to be well clear of those troubled waters.

Although highlights like this and attacks on other warships added considerable interest to mundane activities, for most of the time the members of the B-Dienst earned their keep by collecting frustratingly small pieces of seemingly unimportant information and it took a considerable time before all this could be built into a useful picture. As far as the U-boat Command was concerned, it was important to establish the vital data needed to attack convoys which was potentially far more valuable than tackling lone merchant ships. The B-Dienst worked hard to establish the essential statistics and much to everybody's surprise the necessary information was exceedingly fast in coming. In fact the first U-boat to be directed to a convoy was *U31* (Kptlt Johannes Habekost) when it sunk the 4,040grt freighter *Aviemore* from OB4 (outward-bound from Liverpool) on 16 September 1939. Yet, despite this early success, much painstaking detective work was necessary before the U-boat Command could make use of the collected data. Germany wanted to know the starting and finishing points of convoys, their composition, routes, speed, general rhythms and details about escorts. Knowing the rhythm was vital because there was no point in searching empty seas when a convoy was known to have passed and the next one might not be due for a long time.

As has already been said, much of this information was gleaned from plain language Morse signals, but it was quickly discovered that convoy operations also generated extensive voice messages in what appeared to be non-coded language. Yet making sense of this was most difficult, even for boats with reasonable English speakers on board. Many of these messages could not be picked up in Germany and the flow of words was too fast, even for someone with good school or college English. Consequently the B-Dienst assembled a core of linguists who could be sent out with U-boats for the sole purpose of listening to conversations. These efforts paid dividends before the end of 1939 by making it possible to provide the U-boat Command with daily intelligence reports, which became more valuable as time went on. One big drawback for all the radio intelligence work at the time was that existing recording gear was too delicate, heavy and cumbersome to be carried conveniently in submarines.

While the seemingly insignificant pieces of the grand jigsaw were being snapped into place, to form a fascinating long-term picture of how convoys operated, the B-Dienst also achieved considerable short-term successes. One of these began unexpectedly during the morning of 26 October 1940, when the giant 42,348grt passenger ship, *Empress of Britain*, reported being hit by a bomb from a long-range Focke-Wulf bomber. A short time later came the news of her being taken in tow by one of the escorting destroyers. This suggested a fire, which had been reported earlier, was more serious than Berlin had first imagined. The next useful snippet, from the Admiral in command in the Clyde, told the Germans that tugs and rescue ships were on their way west. Following this, the drama continued in silence in the airwaves until early evening when a report stated the *Empress* was lying on even keel, but the crew had been evacuated and the fire was possibly under control.

The B-Dienst decoded the messages and passed them on to the appropriate authorities but did not know how they might be acted on. U-boat positions were secret enough for the B-Dienst not to be given access to them and it only got to know where individuals were when it intercepted radio messages. In any case, codes coming in from recognisable German sources and addressed to known locations, did not come within the B-Dienst's jurisdiction. On this occasion, *U32* (ObltzS Hans Jenish) was at hand to ram a torpedo into the still floating wreck on 28 October 1940, saving Britain the effort of salvaging it. The first the B-Dienst knew about this was when the tug *Marauder* came on the air saying there had been an explosion aboard the *Empress of Britain*, which started sinking shortly afterwards, some 200 miles west of Malin Head. A few days later Jenish was rewarded for his efforts by being promoted to Kapitänleutnant, but by then he and 33 of his men were already prisoners of war and his boat was lying on the bottom of the Atlantic, having been depth-charged by the destroyers *Harvester* and *Highlander*.

By this time the B-Dienst had made considerable inroads on the convoy problem, supplying positions, routes and times when they were sailing. Tracking them was considerably more difficult. There were only a few transmissions from the convoy once the ships were under way, although the instructions from land-based operation rooms, with changes in route, were easily decipherable. At this stage in the war, most of the battles were taking place in the relatively shallow waters west of Ireland and Scotland and the convoys appeared to head straight into positions occupied by U-boats. It appeared that the Admiralty was expecting them to attack below the surface and was putting too much emphasis on the underwater detector Asdic (sonar).

In addition to the successes, there were also a number of strange mysteries. One of these occurred during August 1940, when 10 ships were attacked by *U37* under Kptlt Victor Oehrn, but only one of them sent a distress signal. The Admiralty's reaction was to dispatch two auxiliary cruisers, suggesting there was a dire shortage of anti-submarine vessels, since these cumbersome ex-merchant ships were hardly agile enough to tackle such small craft as submarines. The question being asked in Germany was: why had only one of the sunk ships used her radio? Later, the post-cruise analysis revealed that four of the targets were sunk with torpedoes, but Oehrn was also rather sick of this weapon. He had started his career with a good number of torpedo failures and as a result used his deck guns to deal with five ships, while another was sunk using the guns and a torpedo. These lengthy bombardments gave the victims ample time for sending distress calls, but possibly Germany failed to pick them up. This made the B-Dienst wonder how and why they could have been missed.

Another strange occurrence took place early in December 1940 when, despite a general order for ships in convoy not to use radio under any circumstances, at least six ships from convoy HX90 sent clear distress calls with positions. The B-Dienst could not determine whether this was a blatant case of disobeying orders, whether the radio operators were under the impression they could send SSS calls or whether the B-Dienst had misunderstood the original order. The problem was in determining whether the calls were genuine or whether they were deliberate hoaxes to draw U-boats away from convoys. The difficult point with this was that such calls did not come in occasionally, but they appeared in vast quantities and some of the SSS distress signals definitely came from areas where there were no U-boats. Sorting out such confusion was most difficult.

The nature of distress calls varied considerably, with many victims not using standard transmission patterns and some forgetting vital pieces of information in the rush. For example, several SSS calls were intercepted without the victim's position. The B-Dienst found it curious that from 100 ships sunk during the summer and autumn of 1940, only 48 sent a distress call at all and only 37 of these gave their names, while 11 remained anonymous. When checking these distress calls with

debriefing details once U-boats were back in port, it became apparent that British warship losses by contrast were broadcast quite regularly and accurately, making it possible to check many of the shooting details in U-boat logs by identifying the target.

The B-Dienst intercepted many clues well in advance of major actions, but despite this the whole process cannot be described as plain sailing. Often there were considerable problems to be solved and no easy conclusions could be drawn from the deciphered words themselves. The whole procedure was very much like piecing together a jigsaw, only to find that vital areas remained as conspicuous holes, without any obvious pieces to fit into them. For example, decrypts gave a complete list of ships' names, cargoes and speeds for convoys SL53 and SLS53 (Freetown in Sierra Leone to UK), but there were no indications of position or of the starting time. Since it was known to be under way, Focke-Wulf reconnaissance bombers were sent out from France to find it and when one of these attacked the 9,333grt British freighter *Apapa*, she obliged by sending a distress call with name, call sign GMSB and the vital position. One of the major problems with joint air and submarine operations was that the Luftwaffe was not terribly good at navigating over featureless water and their reported positions were often not accurate enough for U-boats to home in on. Therefore Admiral Dönitz, the officer commanding U-boats, changed the rules. Instead of prohibiting attacks by aircraft, he told them to annoy merchant ships to induce them into transmitting a report which hopefully would include their position.

This time, the puzzling point in Germany was that *Apapa* had also announced she had left the convoy and joined a different one, so it was not clear where the rest of the merchant ships were. This was later followed by seven clear distress calls from GFZK, which was known to have been the commodore's ship, the British freighter *Nestlea*, but it was not clear whether she was still with the convoy. The Italian submarine *Baracca* under Enrico Bertarelli attacked the British freighter *Lilian Moller*, but even so, the B-Dienst was unable to fill the gaps in the jigsaw it had almost completed.

In addition to keeping tabs on U-boat operations, the B-Dienst confirmed that the prewar pattern of natural damage caused by the elements was still making its presence felt and this powerful force did not discriminate between nationalities. Convoy OB252, for example, was told to make a drastic change in course to avoid an area where there had been intense U-boat activity. The B-Dienst did not know exactly where the U-boats were nor whether they might reach the new position. Yet, even without U-boats present, at least 25 storm damage reports were intercepted and decoded during the next few days. The 5,342grt freighter *Bodnant* reported colliding with the 6,402grt freighter *City of Bedford* and announced her hull was leaking, but she would try to make for Iceland. The other victim asked for help, but did not specify what damage she had received. Not everybody was so lucky to be able to limp to the nearest port. The 4,099grt freighter *Jessmore* stated she was sinking after having collided with an unidentified ship which did not use its radio. The storm was obviously bad and when it abated the sea was covered with thick fog, making it difficult to maintain position in convoy and many ships were scattered across the ocean to fend for themselves. The 10,468grt tanker *W. B. Walker* came on the air in desperation with news of her hull breaking up. Then the B-Dienst lost track of what happened to the crew, but about a week later a signal reported the bows of what had been a tanker to be floating on its own near this position. A tug was sent there, but it proved impossible to get a tow on board and then Germany lost track of what happened with the remains.

The U-boats which managed to get home for Christmas 1940 were greeted with an exceptionally cold New Year when not only the fresh water in the Kiel Canal but also the salty sea froze into a white rockery. Further out, away from the ice, men from both sides suffered unimaginable hardships and no one was surprised by the decrease in U-boat sinking figures. For many, it was a case of struggling on against the elements rather than thinking about attacking. It was hoped the sinking figures would rise once again in spring, but this was not to be. Instead of successes, however, spring brought a chain of disasters which resulted in a number of ace U-boat commanders being lost.

Since the Royal Navy was not shy about using radio, it was often possible for the B-Dienst to provide explanations about what had happened. They did, however, compound a wartime German misconception about Asdic being a listening device rather than sonar. The initials 'HE' had been intercepted frequently and intelligence officers concluded that they stood for Hydrophone Effect, believing, incorrectly, that Britain had introduced a new type of Asdic into service that operated as a sensitive underwater microphone to listen for noises made by U-boats. However, some mysteries remain which cannot be solved, even with radio data from both sides. For example, the destroyer *Wolverine* provided such a constant running commentary of her search for a U-boat, that it was assumed she had sunk *U47* with the heroes of Scapa Flow on board, but when detailed records became available after the war, it was realised that *U47* had used its radio some time after this hunt and that the boat must therefore have succumbed to some other cause. As yet, every explanation offered by historians has been found not to hold water.

So far, the information the B-Dienst had supplied to the U-boat Arm had been useful, but non-essential. During the autumn of 1940, many commanders found it was unnecessary to home in on convoys reported over the radio because they ran into an abundance of targets long before they reached them. This changed in the late spring of 1941, when U-boats were faced mainly with empty seas, plus occasional annoying aircraft and irritating escorts. The big questions being asked in Germany were: where were the convoys and how were they avoiding the U-boats? The B-Dienst confirmed there had been no reduction in the volume of radio traffic, so there was no doubt that convoys were still being assembled on both sides of the Atlantic. In addition to this, a good number of distress calls from ships at sea as a result of natural disasters were still being intercepted. It was assumed that the convoys had to have found new routes around German patrol lines.

One important clue came from several signals to convoy commodores to avoid certain areas where U-boats were thought to be lurking and it was not long before someone suggested the possibility of these warnings coming shortly after a boat in the area had used its radio. This immediately pointed the finger at radio direction finders. Of course, what actually was happening was that Britain was starting to read the secret U-boat code. Although the possibility of Britain having broken into the German code was considered by the U-boat Command, the Naval War Staff refused to believe it, saying the Enigma system was too complicated and could not be defeated. This left Germany searching for some other alternative and, obviously, radio direction finders were one possible culprit.

At this stage of the proceedings, the German leadership created a huge problem for itself, which contributed greatly to the Allied success. Although the B-Dienst had been built up to an impressively high level and supplied a multitude of useful deciphered intercepts, there were not enough intelligence officers to evaluate the results. Rather than comb painstakingly through these intercepts, the U-boat Arm and the Supreme Naval Command did the exact opposite and reduced the number of people in the know about U-boat activities as a means of increasing security. Several spy hunts resulted in a further reduction of the U-boat staff. There was no effective centralised intelligence service and no one looking over the shoulders of the higher commanders to assess the results of their actions.

The B-Dienst was still supplying a continuous flow of interesting general information as well as the specific dates when convoys were sailing. This was deduced from masses of signals floating about while the ships were assembling and then, when everything went quiet, it was assumed the ships had departed. However, this information was not enough when the drama was being played out over the vast area of the Atlantic. It was similar to finding a convoy travelling from, say, Athens to London while all the participants could move no faster than a jogger or a cyclist.

While searching for clues in the airwaves, the B-Dienst also supplied the U-boat Command with the type of

Above: U180 was one of only two specially built ocean-going, long-distance cargo carriers, the design of which was quickly modified to produce the U-Kreuzer or U-Cruiser of Type IXD2. Although these boats had an impressive range and more spacious compartments than the run-of-the-mill type of boat, they were still exceedingly cramped and lacked facilities for carrying specialised intelligence staff. Therefore the evaluation of in-coming messages had to be digested by the commander and watch officers on top of their already over-burdened work load.

information no one there was keen on hearing. In June 1941 the B-Dienst discovered the convoys HX129 and HX130 were the first to be escorted all the way across the Atlantic, an indication that the battles were going to get a great deal harder in the future. This was made clear a short time later when a wolf pack of 11 boats was set up to intercept convoy HX145. Despite being fairly certain of its route, the boats came home empty handed, having failed to find their target.

This news had hardly been digested when an even worse signal shot into the U-boat Headquarters. An aircraft on anti-submarine duty had attacked a U-boat to the south of Iceland, which responded by showing a white flag. The news was unbelievable. Although the U-boat Command obviously knew which boats were in that area, it was still difficult to establish its identity, but at first no one was terribly concerned. It sounded like one of those flaps which would sort themselves out again. After all, this happened at a time when Admiral Dönitz, the U-boat chief, was still saying

aircraft could not hurt submarines. Yet, more worrying news followed a short time later, when the B-Dienst intercepted and deciphered a signal saying four armed trawlers were converging on the spot. Then another signal implied that a warship had also appeared on the scene. Not long before this Britain had introduced a new system preventing ships from giving their names in radio transmissions. Instead they used a reference number, meaning it was exceedingly difficult for Germany to work out exactly which ships it was dealing with. Even so, the B-Dienst was able to discover that some injured men were transferred from the U-boat to one of the British ships and then the airwaves went quiet for a while, in fact while *U570* (Kptlt Hans Rahmlow) was being towed to Iceland. Once this had been achieved, the B-Dienst and cryptanalysts were no longer required. Britain gladly published the news of a U-boat hoisting a white flag in mid-Atlantic, Allied propaganda exploiting the story to the full.

Right:
U154 spent a considerable time in the Central Atlantic and in the Caribbean. The circular aerial of the Metox radar-warning device, sticking up above the conning tower wall by the man on the right, indicates this picture was taken towards the end of the Atlantic activities. Long-range boats, like this Type IXC, had considerable problems coping with intelligence information. Very often situations changed rapidly enough for pre-sailing briefings to be out of date by the time the boat arrived in its operation area. Therefore, a vast number of special messages were broadcast to keep the men informed of what was going on. Yet digesting all this data was most difficult because even these bigger boats did not carry special intelligence officers to cope with the inflow of news.

Chapter 8
Enter the United States

The Japanese attack on Pearl Harbor took place on 7 December 1941 and Germany declared war on the United States on the 11th, but according to Heinz Bonatz, this was not the beginning of America's involvement in the Battle of the Atlantic. Apparently, he felt, international neutrality laws had already been disregarded for a long time. According to these, a neutral country should not participate in a declared conflict, nor help the warring sides, nor allow military forces of either side to pass through its territory, national waters or air space. Yet, despite being so keen on quoting the law as far as German transgressions were concerned, America made a concerted effort to ignore the terms of such international agreements.

Two years earlier, soon after the outbreak of war, it had already become apparent to Berlin that the United States had taken it upon itself to help Britain sink unarmed merchant ships by assuring these would be intercepted by the Royal Navy. One of the most dramatic of such cases involved the giant 32,582grt liner *Columbus*, belonging to Norddeutscher Lloyd of Bremen, which remained in Tampico (Mexico) until the end of 1939. The story of its bid for freedom and attempted return to Germany is told most dramatically by one of her officers, Otto Giese, in his stunning book *Shooting the War*. Even commercial giants such as *Columbus* did not have naval radio intercept officers on board and it is likely her communications room did not even have facilities for tuning into military wavelengths. In any event, Otto Giese did not know what was going on in the airwaves and the first clue of something untoward which would prevent the run back to Germany was deciphered far away in Berlin, on 5 December 1939. This was a signal to all United States ships off Mexico, telling them there were indications that a number of German ships in Tampico were being made ready for putting to sea. At the same time, other plain language, but confusing, messages were being intercepted, such as 'George and Nerolie are worshipping together it goes not too well with Kathleen have no prospects for Lucy be prepared.' Adding a few full stops will make the jumble of words easier to follow. Thus: 'George and Nerolie are worshipping together. It goes not too well with Kathleen. Have no prospects for Lucy. Be prepared.' When some of these words were repeated in other messages, the B-Dienst guessed there was some hidden meaning and not long afterwards discovered that George meant Britain, Nerolie referred to the United States, Kathleen was a blockade breaking run to Germany, and Lucy referred to possible German assistance.

Cryptanalysts were still analysing such messages when it became clear that *Columbus's* bid for freedom was going to be frustrated by the cruiser USS *Tuscaloosa*, which was following a short distance behind and broadcasting its position, together with details of the liner. Not long afterwards a small British destroyer, *Hyperion*, appeared on the horizon and quickly put a shot across the bows of the German giant. This was followed by the instruction for *Columbus* to consider herself captured. However, the men on board had other ideas. The master, Kapitän Willibald Dähne, had already given his key officers written instructions, telling them what to do if an attempt was made to board the ship. Engine room inlet valves were opened, fuel poured over mattresses and the ship set on fire. Very quickly the giant became a raging inferno. A sad end for such a proud ship, but better than handing it over to the opposition. The crew took to the lifeboats and were picked up by USS *Tuscaloosa*.

Such openly hostile action was not restricted to the waters around the United States, nor was this an isolated case. The US cruiser *Omaha* stopped, boarded and captured the freighter *Odenwald* off Brazil on 6 November 1941, a whole month before the attack on Pearl Harbor. The B-Dienst discovered the excuse for this blatant infringement by a neutral country. According to intercepts, the reason given was that the *Odenwald* was suspected of carrying slaves and therefore had to be inspected in a port. There was very little Germany could do about such obvious disregard of international law. In any case by this time it was well known how the United States was not only supplying Britain with war goods but also repairing Royal Navy warships in American shipyards, making it quite plain that neutrality was being disregarded on a wide front.

Heinz Bonatz has mentioned how captured German intercepts were taken away by the victorious Allies after the war for laundering. They were later returned with significant holes in some critical places. So it was difficult for him to determine exactly how far such breaches of neutrality penetrated. Some of the gaps in the records are exceedingly difficult to spot and usually it is only when one is searching for a series of events that one notices the hidden gaps. However, German infringements are far easier to find. One such took place during the early hours of 31 October 1941, when *U552* (Kptlt Erich Topp) torpedoed the United States destroyer *Reuben James*. At first, this was presented as an innocent neutral being viciously attacked, and it was a while before it became clear that the ship was escorting convoy HX156 into a war zone.

Above: These photos by Otto Giese were taken shortly after he had abandoned the already sinking passenger ship *Columbus*. The ship had been scuttled to prevent it falling into Allied hands after a neutral United States cruiser had directed a British warship to intercept the giant.

The media has made the point that the onslaught against Pearl Harbor was unprovoked and totally unexpected. Yet, had researchers looked at the masses of decrypts from intercepted messages, they would have realised the event was not as unexpected as it has often been made out. The German B-Dienst intercepted a warning as early as 16 October 1941, when US shipping in the Pacific was told to be prepared for an attack by Japanese forces. A week later, this was followed by a general prohibition to broadcast in open language. In Berlin it was clear that Britain was also expecting repercussions from Japanese interests, but since a large proportion of the Far East communications were sent by cable telephone lines, it was difficult to analyse exactly what precautions were being taken. However, on 6 November 1941, shipping was warned of a defensive mine barrage protecting Hong Kong, suggesting preparations there had been ongoing for some time. Since there were no German ships anywhere near this area, it suggested Britain was also expecting an attack from the Japanese.

There were other rather strange abnormalities during the few days preceding the surprise attack against Pearl Harbor. The Hawaiian Islands apparently did not heed the warning sent to ships in the Pacific and there were no indications in the airwaves of this massive naval base being put on a higher level of alertness. So, the experts in Berlin were asking themselves: why was American shipping in the Pacific warned of an imminent Japanese attack, but why was the military apparently taking no significant precautions?

Although the events in the Pacific were of general interest to Germany, the real challenge for the B-Dienst came a little later when attention was turned on America's east coast, to establish what war preparations were being taken in the Atlantic. In 1939, shortly after the outbreak of war, the United States had declared this area to be a neutrality zone and Hitler, not wanting to provoke them, prohibited U-boats from operating there. This meant the Kriegsmarine had very little intelligence of shipping patterns in those far-flung waters despite the high level of activity. This lack of information was broken on 12 January 1942, when the British freighter *Cyclops* sent a distress call with her call sign GPZK from a position off New York, an indication to the B-Dienst of Allied activity in the area, and that the German receivers had not broken! The previous four weeks had been disconcerting. Nothing unusual had been picked up and the B-Dienst was wondering whether it was missing out on something, the absence of any conspicuous war

Above: The U-boat Operations Room at Kernével near Lorient in France. The map rack in the background is of special significance because towards the beginning of the war, charts were pinned to the wall. It was the fear of spies gaining valuable information which resulted in them being hidden from view. The U-boat Chief, Karl Dönitz, can be identified by the Vice Admiral's sleeve rings. On the left is Kptlt Herbert Schultze of *U48*, the most successful boat of the war, and in the background, fourth from the front, is Kptlt Fuhrmann, Flag Lieutenant from 1941-3. Such briefings and debriefings were a major tool for keeping sea-going officers up-to-date with latest developments.

Right:
A large ocean-going
U-boat ploughs its way
through heavy
breakers.

preparations being puzzling. Intelligence officers even suggested that the defence of the east coast could be controlled by a secret telephone network, rather than by radio. Germany desperately wanted to know what protective measures were being taken and how convoy defences were being organised but, instead of this, the airwaves continued as they had done in peacetime, with harbourmasters even announcing departure and expected arrival times of ships. It was only when the absence of any war preparations was confirmed by the first U-boats of Operation Paukenschlag — the initial campaign against the United States — that this news finally sunk in. Up to then the B-Dienst was under the impression many of the American broadcasts could be deliberate attempts to mislead the opposition.

The initial pickings in American coastal waters were unexpectedly rich and the services of the B-Dienst were not required to help the U-boats find targets, although everybody guessed it would not be long before attacks became considerably more difficult to launch. Therefore, as much exploratory work as was possible was carried out. The Radio Monitoring Service listened with interest to how the first defences were organised, how convoys were formed and Germany gained a generally good understanding of the patterns of the area. Much of this detective work followed a boring routine, but there were a few interesting cases. One of these was highlighted on 19 February, when KDUK, the 7,460grt freighter *Mokihana*, sent a distress call, saying she was being chased by a submarine. There were no known U-boats near this area and therefore officers immediately pricked up their ears, but nothing more was heard. It took a considerable effort for the B-Dienst in Berlin to discover from the U-boat headquarters in Kernével near Lorient in France that *U161* (Kptlt Albrecht Achilles) had been responsible for the attack, but his position had not been passed on earlier in order to maintain secrecy. The decline in sinkings achieved by U-boats throughout 1941 had resulted in several spy hunts and at that time it was decided not to pass on U-boat positions to other naval authorities unless it was vital for the recipient to be informed. *Mokihana*, incidentally, was salvaged but sunk for a second time on 4 May 1942 by *U125* (Kptlt Ulrich Folkers).

Another curiosity occurred later in the year when the Italian U-boat *Barbarigo* (Enzo Grossi) reported attacking the 33,000-ton USS *Mississippi*. The word 'battleship' in the brief message made the operators on duty sit up, but they never discovered exactly what happened. Somehow in the darkness of the night, the Italians confused the 925-ton corvette *Petunia* for this massive monster, but the news did keep the B-Dienst on tenterhooks for some time until the identity of the tiny corvette was revealed. A similar misunderstanding had occurred more than a year earlier when *U99* (Kptlt Otto Kretschmer) was reported as attacking the British battleship *Nelson*. The U-boat was hardly back in port when the Commander-in-Chief wanted to know exactly what had happened. Kretschmer looked puzzled at first and then laughed. He had been chasing what he thought was a British submarine and it was not until the torpedo exploded bang on target that he realised the silhouette of the conning tower had actually been a rather solid rock off Scotland's west coast. He had laughed off this embarrassing episode by ordering the signal 'Rock torpedoed' to be transmitted in Morse code at the end of a regular report and the German word for rock is '*Felsen*', which was misunderstood at the receiving end.

By the autumn of 1942, the B-Dienst had been earning its laurels by providing the U-boat Command with a good flow of useful information as it was able to decipher much of the Convoy Cipher, introduced in June 1941, which the Allied navies were using at this time to communicate with each other in the Atlantic. The assembly of convoys, as well as their starting positions and departure times, were often intercepted, making it possible to assemble wolf packs across the anticipated path. In one example, the information supplied by the B-Dienst enabled the Veilchen wolf pack to be assembled so that convoy SC107 would run directly into the middle of its U-boats' patrol line shortly after leaving New York for London in early November 1942. During the next few nights, 34 attacks took place against the 27 ships of the convoy, and its Canadian escort group, which resulted in 19 being sunk or damaged. Bearing in mind that none of these boats would have made contact with the convoy, had Allied signals not been intercepted and deciphered in time, it meant the B-Dienst had certainly become a vital contributor to the Battle of the Atlantic. However, the problem was that in the majority of convoys, these ships vanished in the vastness of the ocean and route changes broadcast to convoys once they were under way resulted in many wolf packs being avoided completely or the merchant ships running into only the extreme end of a patrol line. This was achieved despite it being at a time when Bletchley Park, the British deciphering centre, could not read the U-boat code. The three-wheel Enigma machine was changed for a four-wheel device in February 1942 and Britain did not get back into the new system until after men from *Petard* captured such a machine, together with the necessary code books, from *U559* (Kptlt Hans Heidtmann) on 30 October 1942.

The astonishing point about the Battle of the Atlantic was that the number of U-boats at sea reached 70 in July 1942 and then climbed to 100 for September, and remained at this fantastically high level until June of the following year, although the convoy battles did not peak until the massive engagements of March 1943. Although such vast numbers of U-boats at sea resulted in many merchant ships being sunk, the performance of individual boats dropped most dramatically. This was largely due to Germany not having provided its major

Above and opposite: U67, which was commissioned by the ace 'Ajax' Bleichrodt on 22 January 1941. Bleichrodt said that too much contradictory information flooded out of the radio room, making it difficult to keep abreast with what was going on and most often it was best to ignore the messages or switch the radio off. It seems highly likely that this picture was taken during artillery practice with the 105mm quick-firing deck gun, rather than during actual action.

weapon with decent aerial reconnaissance, meaning that U-boat patrol lines were more or less assembled entirely from B-Dienst decrypts, rather than from positions based on definite sightings.

Although history books tend to give the impression that 1942 was a bleak period for the Allies, it must be borne in mind that the vast majority of U-boats never came within sight of merchant ships. Far greater numbers were pushed under by aircraft or by escorts long before they could even contemplate an attack. The astonishing point about this performance was that the B-Dienst actually provided the German leaders with the vital clues about how this was being done, but no one in Germany took any notice. Although Germany was able to read a high proportion of Allied signals during the height of the Battle of the Atlantic, a single convoy battle often

resulted in U-boats making more than a hundred radio transmissions, which were picked up by Allied high frequency direction finders aboard ships, making it possible to determine the direction from which they were coming and radar was then used to find the boat on the surface. Thus, radio had become the vital key to the Battle of the Atlantic for both sides and would ultimately play a part in Germany's defeat in the Atlantic. From June 1943 the flow of information to B-Dienst in relation to the Battle of the Atlantic was severely reduced when the Allies replaced the Convoy Cipher with Naval Cipher No 5 for communications between the British, US and Canadian navies in the Atlantic, which was in turn replaced in November 1943 by the Combined Cipher System, based on the Typex (Type X) machine, which the Germans found virtually impossible to break into.

Above: A High Frequency Direction Finder (HF/DF) — known as Huff Duff — on top of the main mast of HMS *Plymouth* at the Warship Preservation Trust in Birkenhead (near Liverpool) in England. This type of aerial was used to home in on U-boat radio transmissions during the war.

Chapter 9
The End of the U-boat War

The number of U-boats at sea at any one time increased dramatically throughout 1942 until September, when it reached the psychological barrier of 100 and from then on it remained at or above that high level until the summer of the following year. Historians have repeatedly told us how exceedingly bleak this period was for the Allies, with the U-boats almost winning the Battle of the Atlantic, but this view is not supported by the general picture to emerge from countless decrypts. As far as the B-Dienst was concerned, U-boat successes appeared to be like a blind chicken finding corn simply because there were enough grains scattered around. The vast majority of boats were not achieving a great deal and the number of ships sunk per U-boat at sea was dropping dramatically. These meagre results were partly due to boats operating a long way from home, meaning they spent considerably more time travelling to and from their operational areas, rather than attacking. The B-Dienst was achieving considerable success in locating the assembly points for convoys, but immense problems

developed once the ships were under way. For most of the time there were no clues at all about their speed or direction, making tracking difficult as these two criteria had to be guessed. As a result of this, despite the large numbers of U-boats at sea, the majority did not make contact with suitable targets.

Winter blues were adding considerable boredom to the mundane routines within the B-Dienst, when, in February 1943, an Allied signal giving the positions of wolf packs was cracked. This had hardly been passed on to the U-boat Operations Department, when an urgent enquiry about its source bounced back. Could this information have come from a German radio? The answer was negative. The B-Dienst confirmed that not only had the signal originated somewhere in the United Kingdom, but it had also been in the British Merchant Navy Code. (Although the British had by this time replaced the Merchant Navy Code with the Merchant Ships Code, the Germans still referred to it as the Merchant Navy Code.) The next question was how

Above: Men relaxing on the winter garden or conservatory to the rear of the conning tower of *U219* with the naval ensign fluttering in breeze.

Above: U441 catches some spray from a calm sea. One would be tempted to suggest the boat is preparing to attack the two ships on the horizon, but the officer of the watch would not have allowed a photographer on the upper deck during serious action. Therefore this picture was more likely to have been taken while sailing in or out of a safe port. Type VII boats were fitted with an 88mm quick-firing deck gun, as can be seen in the foreground.

Britain could have determined these positions so accurately. This had hardly been uttered, when KptzS Eberhard Godt (Deputy Head of U-boat Operations) suggested that Germany's own code had been compromised. It was obvious to him that someone had to be reading the Enigma cipher (and we now know that Godt was right). This was so serious that an inquiry was immediately set up to examine each individual case in detail. The results came quickly. Experts said the U-boat code was impossible to crack and concluded that every position had been determined either by a sighting from an aircraft or surface ship or deduced from attacks or worked out with the aid of radar. Consequently, the U-boat Command was talked out of the idea of the code being no longer secure and the matter was dropped.

The discussions between the U-boat Operations Department and the Supreme Naval Command about how these positions might have been determined hardly affected the B-Dienst, which was busy keeping tabs on convoy movements. A major opportunity came early in March, by kind permission of the atrocious weather. An eastbound convoy had been detected in Canadian waters and a wolf pack was assembled in its path, but the position of the merchant ships was not known, despite a number of course changes having been intercepted. The U-boats were lucky, though it did not seem so at first. The convoy was sighted briefly before a storm blew up and was quickly lost again during the appalling weather. However, the severity of the weather resulted in a number of ships being scattered far and wide. At first,

simple calculations in Germany with the convoy's speed suggested all of the U-boats were likely to miss it, even if the weather mellowed. Yet, this was not the case. During the dark, early hours of 7 March, *U230* (Kptlt Paul Siegmann) reported torpedoing the Ellerman Line's freighter SS *Egyptian*. This provided an approximate position of the convoy and made it possible for other U-boats to close in. *U230*'s location on the German naval grid chart was quickly confirmed by the victim sending her position while asking for help. Now Germany had a fairly good fix on convoy HX228.

Following this, several more stragglers blown out of the convoy were sunk and six U-boats actually found the main group but an intensification of the storm to Force 10, with fierce snow and hail showers, prevented any thoughts of attacking. The term 'straggler', which was always used for any ship which had dropped behind a convoy, suggests that such ships simply followed the same course as before but at some distance behind the main body, but this was not the case. All ships were given special straggler routes to follow if they could not keep up, to make it difficult for an enemy to determine the location of the main convoy from spotting a lone ship.

When the storm subsided there came one of those tense periods when nobody at the B-Dienst had any inclination to go off duty, even at the end of their shift. This excitement started with the interception of a sighting report from the British destroyer *Harvester* (Commander A. A. Tait), with the escort to convoy HX228. Apparently her target had time to dive, but was brought back to the surface by some well-placed depth charges. The U-boat then identified itself as *U444* (ObltzS Albert Langfeld) and this was followed by another British signal saying the destroyer had rammed and then run over the U-boat. In Berlin the staff almost held their breaths when they realised that somehow the two had become locked together for 15 minutes or so, putting both in a dire predicament. Having freed themselves, but still nursing their wounds, the adversaries seemed to have gone their own ways, although it was not clear whether *U444* had been sunk or not. As it turned out *U444* remained crippled on the surface until the French corvette *Aconit* (Capitaine de frégate J. Lavasseur), which had been sent to help *Harvester*, rammed the U-boat. In the meantime, *Harvester* had been discovered and sunk by *U432* (Kptlt Hermann Eckhardt), but smoke attracted *Aconit*, which then destroyed this U-boat as well. Once again the weather worsened to winds of Force 10, accompanied by heavy snow and hail, making further attacks on the convoy impossible and this gave the U-boat Command no choice other than to withdraw from the action because the majority of boats were now running dangerously low on fuel.

Next, the B-Dienst achieved one of its major coups. On 12 March 1943 the cryptanalysts decoded the entire course orders for a convoy being assembled at Halifax in Nova Scotia. The remaining U-boats from the previous action were refuelled at sea and supplemented with a high number of newcomers to form two wolf packs of almost 20 boats. Germany did not know it at the time but the fast convoy HX229 with 40 ships was about to set out on a similar course to the previous slow convoy SC122 with 54 ships and gradually overtake it to form the target for the biggest convoy battle of the war. The first snag in the hunt came at a time when everything was thought to be running smoothly. Suddenly, without warning, the B-Dienst intercepted an order to change course at Point J, a location which had not been mentioned in the original instructions. Obviously the ship masters had been given additional information to that mentioned in the initial radio message, making it look as if the merchantmen were going to slip through the net once more.

The U-boat Command had no alternative other than to continue as best it could and hope that its calculations would still bring the packs into contact with the convoy.

Above: A Type VII U-boat, heading out into the unknown. Although the B-Dienst produced all manner of useful information, most of these essential details were broadcast to boats while they were at sea, and for much of the time Britain could also read the U-boat code and was able to put Allied convoys one step ahead.

Chapter 10
The Soviet Union: The Coastal Regions

Despite the non-aggression pact concluded with the Soviets only two weeks before the beginning of World War 2, naval radio surveillance of Soviet activities continued. The first wartime demands for naval intelligence about Russia were made a few days after the launch of the German invasion of Poland. Army generals approached the B-Dienst to ask how Soviet forces invading Poland from the east were likely to react when they met German troops. Was the Red Army going to stop once it reached the limits secretly agreed with Germany. Or was it likely to try squashing Germany as well? The B-Dienst was able to calm jittery nerves by suggesting this was unlikely, as there was no evidence in the airwaves for such a stance. These inferences, drawn from intercepts, were later proved to be correct and the Eastern Front settled into an uneasy truce for the first winter of World War 2, but the B-Dienst continued providing enough evidence to suggest neither side trusted the other.

After the winter freeze 1940 started with an impressive Soviet exercise, almost as if stiff muscles from hibernation needed to be flexed carefully back into action. This gave the B-Dienst an excellent opportunity to study what was actually being practised. Although much of the Russian thinking remained a mystery, the results did show that the few German naval units in the Baltic could not contain their impressive firepower, if it ever came to a serious crisis. This had hardly been realised when evidence appeared in the airwaves of similar thinking on the other side. It seemed as if the Russians were worried about the possibility of an invasion from the west and fearful of superior naval forces hitting them from the sea. These discoveries had hardly been committed to paper, when large-scale defensive mining activities revealed themselves. Britain had given ample warning for the creation of its explosive barricades, but no such notification was forthcoming from Russia, making the B-Dienst think the interceptors were missing vital messages. It appeared that quite large sea areas were being blocked off without any regard to shipping. Several possible explanations were offered by German intelligence officers and these were still being discussed when Russian radio stations belatedly broadcast details of the prohibited areas. This suggested it was a case of one authority not knowing what another was doing and such thoughts were confirmed by arguments, reprimands and threats in the airwaves.

The quarrels between sea-going commanders and their land-based authorities made the interpretation of signals most difficult. Often ships were simply not doing what was being asked of them and this made German analysts think they had misunderstood the original instructions. It took a while to realise that there were times when there was no correlation at all between orders and what was being carried out. The Russians had also started using several different names or identification numbers for the same ship at the same time and the B-Dienst never fully understood how this was supposed to work. Different authorities seemed to use different names for the same units. Finding this rather confusing, the Germans abandoned the Russian identification systems and created their own. This gave rise to terms such as *Zerstörer 1, 2* and so forth (*Zerstörer* = Destroyer) which were quickly abbreviated to *Z1, Z2*, etc. This worked quite well, as long as the B-Dienst was merely collecting information about Soviet units, but later, when it came to evaluations of actions with similarly titled German ships, it became too difficult to differentiate between nationalities and many Russian units were mistaken for Germans. As a result, the B-Dienst changed the system once more and allocated letters instead of numbers.

Since they were technically on the same side as Russia in 1940, the German Naval High Command was able to ask permission for a freighter to travel along the Siberian Sea route from Norway to the Bering Strait. The ship in question was actually a disguised warship (the smallest auxiliary cruiser, *Komet* under Konteradmiral Robert Eyssen) and it was important for the Russians not to discover the true identity of the ship so incriminating evidence was hidden below decks. The first ship to have navigated the whole length of the Siberian Sea passage in one season had achieved this only a few years earlier, so this was indeed a venture into the unknown. *Komet* was especially prepared by having her bows and hull strengthened with additional steel plates and tree trunks to prevent them from being crushed by ice.

In addition to permission to travel through the Siberian Sea, it was also necessary to have support from Russian icebreakers, so plenty of planning was necessary before *Komet* finally left Gotenhafen (Gdynia) on 3 July 1940, disguised as the freighter *Donau*. A month later she was anchored by the approaches to the Matochkin Strait, a narrow channel between the northern and southern parts of Novaya Zemlya, waiting for escort through exceptionally heavily iced seas. The Germans had chosen a diabolical summer for their expedition, but the icebreakers *Lenin* and *Stalin* finally arrived to embark upon what must have been one of the most epic sea voyages of all times. For the first time in history a non-Russian ship was attempting to pass through the icy Siberian Sea in one season, without overwintering, and by sailing against the direction of ice flow.

The B-Dienst kept an ear open for transmissions from the '*Donau*' and thus could inform the Supreme Naval Command when she reached the most northerly point of her route towards the end of the month. It was also possible to tell the admirals that harmony was not included in the escorting deal and arguments were getting stronger by the day. There was still some considerable distance to go when the Russian authorities ordered the ships to stop. However, ice conditions were getting better and Eyssen took matters into his own hands. Pretending not to understand, he made off on his own in a desperate bid to reach the open waters of the Bering Strait before even worse conditions locked his ship into a frozen grip. The B-Dienst felt relieved when he signalled he had got through and there must have been some satisfaction in Berlin and aboard *Komet* when the icebreakers reported being stuck in ice. Apparently, by obeying the orders to wait, they had been locked into freshly freezing water and were now unable to release themselves, even with the help of explosives. This left them with no alternative other than to remain there until the spring thaw of the following year. *Komet* had certainly had a narrow escape.

Germany launched the invasion of the Soviet Union on 22 June 1941. At the time this came as a surprise to many observers around the world, yet the B-Dienst had been finding ample evidence of both sides making considerable preparations for some time and it seemed to the B-Dienst personnel as if Germany's move was a case of one side jumping before the other. Radio monitors had watched a definite increase in Russian frontier defences and collected evidence of coastal gun emplacements being put on higher levels of readiness. On top of this, Soviet shipping was told to report all sightings, and further specific orders were being issued almost continuously to naval units. This made the Germans think Russia was preparing for action in the Black Sea and Baltic, but not in the cold waters of the Arctic, where there was little German naval activity.

At this time, activities in the Black Sea were more of general interest to the B-Dienst and its main energy was directed towards a possible threat in the Baltic. This was indeed a major worry. The Soviets had two battleships, three cruisers, about 20 destroyers, over 30 minesweepers and almost 50 motor torpedo boats, as well as a mass of smaller craft all identified in the Gulf of Finland. Even more threatening was a fleet of well

Above: Although this looks similar to photographs taken by Otto Giese from the blockade breaker *Anneliese Essberger*, these pictures of auxiliary cruiser *Komet* have come from the Walter Schöppe collection in the U-boot-Archiv. This shows Germany's smallest ghost cruiser in the Pacific, after having become the first non-Russian ship to have negotiated the entire length of the Siberian Sea Passage in one season. The B-Dienst was instrumental in tracking the ship's movements and intercepted numerous messages to and from her Russian icebreaking assistants.

Above: Walter Schöppe has annotated these photos with pen, saying 'Russian Icebreaker of the Stalin Class in pack-ice' and 'A heavy Russian icebreaker of the Stalin Class in 9-10 ball [ie heavy] pack-ice'. It is not certain whether these show the icebreaker which helped *Komet* through the Siberian Sea Passage, or whether it is a similar type of ship on some other occasion, but the pictures illustrate the type of ship which made this fantastic voyage possible.

over 50 submarines. It looked as if this number could almost reach 70, but it was difficult to determine exactly how many were operational. The Navy was very much helped by the B-Dienst's detailed dossier, which made it possible to counterbalance this impressive firepower with the minimum of resources.

Although the Black Sea was initially hardly of interest to the German Navy, the B-Dienst had been covering it and the surrounding area for some time and noted how Soviet surface forces were being called back to their ports. While this was still going on, mine barrages were laid outside their harbours and submarines were sent to patrol the shores of both Bulgaria and Romania. Not long afterwards increased mining activities were detected in the Baltic as well. The rapid eastward advance of the German military resulted in Russia shrinking, but the Kriegsmarine was still concerned about the destructive firepower bottled up in the far eastern reaches of what they called the 'Finnish Bathtub' and it was not long before steps were taken to make sure it could not be unleashed. To achieve this, Germany took a page from the Russian notebook and laid a dense mine barrage across the entrance to the Gulf of Finland.

By 1942, this had turned into a most impressive barrier, but there was ample evidence to suggest that Russian submarines were making a considerable effort to find ways through it. However, regular German patrols along the western extremities prevented the Russian minesweepers from clearing passages through the danger areas. Intercepts made it clear that virtually all of this activity was of a low-key nature, since no supportive backup for naval operations could be detected. However, the nature of these signals also suggested the Russians had not capitulated and were making good use of the confinement by overhauling ships and machinery. This convinced the B-Dienst that the mine barrage was likely to face an even bigger threat in 1943.

German forces may have got into the suburbs of Leningrad, but they did not manage to take possession of the harbours nor of the shipyards there. Bombing and artillery bombardment created widespread destruction and almost starved the inhabitants into submission, but those appalling hardships did not break the resolve of the survivors. Every effort was made to launch a major offensive as soon as the ice permitted the movement of shipping in the spring of 1943. By that time, the B-Dienst had identified at least 25 operational submarines and dragged massive nets with explosives attached into the obvious routes through the minefield, to prevent Russian forces from breaking through.

It looked as if the Russian onslaught on that important minefield was planned most methodically. Submarines were discovered to be leaving base at the rate of one per day and details of their routes were regularly intercepted, but the B-Dienst did not find any evidence of any having passing through the barrier. German submarine hunters were active on the open Baltic side, but the B-Dienst winced at the number of reported successes: the German crews were often inexperienced and wasted valuable depth charges on the many wrecks in these shallow waters. There were certainly no indications in the airwaves of the majority of their targets being operational submarines. Even if messages were not deciphered, each genuine victim usually left a trail of identifiable signals, which usually ended abruptly with a distress call. Since this was missing, officers could only conclude the majority of targets had to be wrecks. In fact the Russians were even more prone to this mistake than the Germans and later reported a constant stream of attacks on U-boats in the Gulf of Finland. The B-Dienst knew full well there were none there until 1944 and therefore knew such claims were nothing more than wishful thinking.

The main worry for 1944 did not come from Russian naval forces, but from a build-up of air power on newly created bases along the coast. The year started with an unusually early spring, making shipping movements possible as early as February. When operations began, wave after wave of Russian aircraft appeared until the German ships had consumed all their ammunition and the crews were totally exhausted, to be annihilated because there was no longer any energy to keep aircraft at bay. From then on the B-Dienst had little positive contribution to make and was reduced to keeping fairly accurate records of the German demise in the Baltic, but even this became increasingly difficult as radio stations had to be evacuated.

The Polar Seas

The Polar seas had seen considerable small-scale exploratory activities since before the beginning of the 20th century. Several nations had launched major Polar expeditions, there were coal mining activities on Spitzbergen and the Russians had set up a number of radio stations in extremely isolated locations. Some of these sent regular weather reports, while others seemed to do nothing more than provide the occasional evidence of the staff there still being alive. Many of these outposts continued their business whilst the Germans advanced deep in Soviet Arctic territory. Spitzbergen was forcibly evacuated by British and Canadian forces, but the radio station there was kept operational afterwards to give the impression that nothing had happened.

One common characteristic of all military activities in the Arctic was that the vast majority of units had to operate totally independently, without any form of backup, and therefore little use was made of radio. The initially limited action up there even did without the usual need to provide a running commentary of what was going on. There was little interference from HQs, and intercept stations did not become too deeply involved. Of course, monitoring Arctic traffic was made considerably easier for the B-Dienst by having set up several radio stations in northern Norway shortly after the German invasion of that country.

Yet, despite the lack of radio activity in the Arctic, the B-Dienst made a considerable effort to establish what was going on in the White Sea and around the Murmansk coast. German ships called at these ports until the summer of 1940 and therefore provided ample knowledge of harbour and military installations, but the intelligence officers knew relatively little about the naval forces there. Less than 10 destroyers were identified, plus about 15 submarines, a few patrol boats and well over 100 military aircraft. The already overworked German High Command could not make this a priority, however, because the Germans themselves had no significant naval units in the north of Norway to counterbalance this threat. This situation started heating up during the summer of 1941 and the first signs of trouble came on 13 July when Russian forces announced an attack on a German submarine far up in the bitter north. It would appear that the torpedo missed, but the subsequent depth-charge attack had been successful. Unable to tie this to a known U-boat, the B-Dienst dismissed this signal as fantasy.

The first positive radio news came on 10 August 1941, when ObltzS Eberhard Hoffmann (*U451*) reported sinking a destroyer. Actually, he hit the 441-ton corvette *SKR-27* (Zhemchug) and his radio operator signed off as *U154*, making the B-Dienst wonder whether this was some type of deception. However, this was not the start of the action in the Polar seas. *U652* (ObltzS Georg-Werner Fraatz) had already sunk the armed steam trawler RT-70 four days earlier some 10 kilometres from Cape Teriberka, but maintained radio silence. The Russians made their first attack on 12 September 1941, sinking the 459grt ferry *Ottar Jarl* off northern Norway. The general picture to emerge was of the majority of Russian crews being poorly trained, and virtually all their attacks ended with torpedoes missing their targets. The B-Dienst could quickly confirm this was definitely a case of failing to train men in attacking techniques because the Russians showed incredible tenacity when it came to getting home in damaged ships and made a terrific effort to bring back seriously battered wrecks which would have been better off at the bottom of the ocean.

The gulf between radio signals and reality increased as time went on. The B-Dienst found no evidence of many reported events ever having happened, although they were proclaimed to have been great victories at the time. Heinz Bonatz cites several such cases of not just confusing a corvette for a destroyer or even a destroyer for a cruiser, but far greater discrepancies. Some of these misidentifications can be put down to the weather — fog or blinding snowstorms hiding actuality — but others must have been the result of a fanciful imagination or gross over-exaggeration. For example, on 5 July 1942,

the submarine *UK21* reported to have shot a salvo of torpedoes at the battleship *Tirpitz* off northern Norway and heard two definite detonations. The commanding officer was immediately proclaimed as Hero of the Soviet Union, but despite keeping an ear open to any information from *Tirpitz*, no more news was forthcoming and much later it was established that nobody aboard the battleship heard the explosions or even noticed an attack. Ten days later Soviet radio announced a strike against a heavily guarded German convoy, claiming to have sunk several ships. The B-Dienst was rather interested because there were no corresponding broadcasts from the German side and there were times when it was thought the interception of the Soviet messages' system was no longer functioning properly. So, once again, post-mortem discussions showed nothing had been lost and no one even recorded having been hit by anything.

It was not terribly long before Britain showed an interest in the Polar sea routes and warships were sent to the north Russian ports on exploratory expeditions to pave the way for further co-operation. This progress was revealed by a number of land-based radio stations transmitting in British code, suggesting the Royal Navy had established its own communications centres near Murmansk and in the White Sea area. Large British warships were discovered off north Russia, but Germany did not have the necessary firepower to challenge any of them and the few U-boats up there were usually beaten by the most appalling weather. The first Allied convoys ran with little interference from the German Navy, although the Luftwaffe took a more serious interest and attempted a number of successful bombing operations against this shipping. That is not to say there was no German naval activity at all, but it was more spasmodic rather than a concerted attempt to stop the merchant traffic. In August 1941, the first of the by now famous PQ and QP convoys got through unscathed.

Kola Bay near Murmansk was the destination of many of the Arctic convoys. This view of a convoy sheltering in the Kola inlet was taken from the flightdeck of escort carrier HMS *Fencer*. IAL

Chapter 11
The Mediterranean

First, to put the Mediterranean into the perspective of time: Italy declared war on Britain and France on 10 June 1940, just a few days before the German–French armistice was signed on the 22nd, and then surrendered on 8 September 1943, when a good proportion of its military joined the Allies in the war against Germany. Spain remained neutral throughout the war, resisting pressure to become involved. However, the Spanish authorities did not prevent German military activities as long as they remained hidden from British eyes and there were no complaints. Consequently a number of German projects were carried out in Spain under cover or in the guise of ordinary commercial enterprises.

The first U-boat operation into the Mediterranean took place towards the end of 1939, when *U26* (Korvkpt Klaus Ewerth) carried out a reconnaissance of the Gibraltar area, but everybody was so scared of being detected by radio direction finders that there was no evidence of this in the ether. Following this, as the possibility grew of Spain, Italy and Turkey joining the war on the German side, British radio activities in the Mediterranean became more intense, with dire warnings of severe retribution if there were any signs of neutrality being broken in the German favour. The B-Dienst was keeping tabs on general British proceedings and established that the location of their main military command centre in the Mediterranean area was being moved to Alexandria in Egypt following the declaration of war by the Italians in June 1940. Late in 1940, it received information that things were becoming jittery enough for the Royal Navy to detach two heavy units, probably battleships, from the North Atlantic convoy routes and one from the Indian Ocean to support activities in the Mediterranean (in November the British Mediterranean Fleet had been augmented by the battleship *Barham* and cruisers *Berwick* and *Glasgow*). This was indeed a considerable sacrifice because German surface raiders had started wreaking havoc with

Above: One way to communicate with men working on deck or when two small boats came close enough together was to use the so-called 'Whisper Bag' or megaphone, as seen here aboard an Italian submarine. These essential pieces of equipment consisted purely of a funnel made from metal sheeting. The man holding the megaphone is Carlo Feccia di Cossato.

Above: U617 under the command of Albrecht Brandi in Pola, in the Mediterranean. The T-shaped device behind the man in the middle is a rotatable head of an early underwater sound detector. Water is a good conductor of sound and engine noises could usually be heard over longer distances than the maximum field of view from the top of the conning tower. Wave noises and the U-boat's own engines prevented such gear from working well while the boat was on the surface, even when the sound detector heads were located at the bottom of the submarine but they were used more successfully when submerged. The wires with the thick insulators, running at an angle from the bows to the top of the conning tower, served as fastening for safety harnesses in rough weather and as a radio aerial. Sticking up from the deck are two retractable bollards for attaching the mooring ropes.

merchant shipping and unprotected convoys were especially vulnerable targets, even for poorly armed auxiliary cruisers.

Germany's first move shortly after the outbreak of war in the field of radio monitoring in the Mediterranean was to establish liaison channels with the Italians. Indeed, this was one of the major tasks assigned to Korvkpt Heinz Bonatz before he was appointed as head of the Funkbeobachtungsdienst (B-Dienst). As has already been said, this co-operation worked much better than the by now famous operational problems of the two countries' forces at the front. In Berlin it was felt the military should not get itself into a position where German forces were going to be controlled by Italian commanders and therefore the Mediterranean became a theatre of war where not only the three main German services (army, navy and air force) had to work in close proximity to each other, but at the same time they had to cope with two nations, speaking two different languages, with two sets of commanders, going along side by side into situations where they could potentially mess things up for each other. The contrasting foreign policies of the two countries caused even further friction between the front line commanders, but this hardly ever penetrated

into the field of radio monitoring, where Heinz Bonatz was most impressed with the Italians' performance.

Today, the Mediterranean is a favourite holiday destination for many North Europeans, but during the 1930s those southern beaches were rather difficult to reach from the majority of German cities, and this remoteness was reflected by Berlin not taking an early interest in the region. The B-Dienst did keep abreast with information by compiling detailed dossiers for various departments, but most of this was picked up from open broadcasts, foreign newspapers and other public sources, rather than from deciphering secret codes. In many ways it was curiosity, rather than dire need, which drove the Germans to explore the radio traffic of the Mediterranean. This stand-off view slowly dissolved, with the Naval High Command first showing an interest in the radio stations at Gibraltar. Such exploratory work would be of great value later on, when German forces were being drawn into the Mediterranean in 1941 and centres under British control such as Egypt and Malta were becoming key thorns in the flesh. The first U-boats arrived under such a thick cloud of secrecy that virtually no one, other the individual commanders and their necessary land-based support structure, knew this point, all the B-Dienst could deduce was that there had been an assault, and it took a while to realise it was a cunning hit-and-run strike rather than an air raid or bombardment from the sea. The British battleships *Queen Elizabeth* and *Valiant*, as well as the Norwegian tanker *Sagona*, had large holes torn in their sides, but the Royal Navy kept up a façade to prevent anyone from recognising the damage. This was a purely cosmetic exercise for observers on the ground or in the air and no serious attempt was made to hide the damage in the abundant flow of radio signals, making it easy for the B-Dienst to discover all three ships were lying in shallow water on even keel. Later, more detailed assessments by German intelligence indicated that the entire battle squadron of the Mediterranean Fleet would be out of action for some while. The B-Dienst even learned how the human torpedoes managed to get into the port. They had just been dropped off by the Italian submarine *Scire* when the net defences were opened for three destroyers. Besides sinking the three ships in shallow water, the destroyer *Jervis* was also damaged, but this daring raid did not have lasting effects as the ships were ready for action again some months later. Air reconnaissance produced photographs of the big ships in dry dock and six months later there was radio evidence of *Queen Elizabeth* transmitting from the Red Sea. This sparked off a photo reconnaissance flight to confirm the dry docks and harbour at Alexandria were empty. The damage must have been repaired.

One problem with the radio war in the Mediterranean was that the period between leaving port and something happening was usually short enough for there not to be enough time between intercepting signals, decoding them, sending forecasts to the appropriate authorities and the action taking place. So, rather than using intercepted messages for forecasting events, the information acquired formed the basis for a news service, with the B-Dienst providing the latest information on what had just happened. In many cases this was quite convenient because the majority of the German units in the Mediterranean were small boats — U-boats, motor torpedo boats or other auxiliaries — which did not radio home very often. MTBs had been brought south by transporting them along the European river and canal system. A good number of these small boats did not have full-time radio operators and, in any case, when it came to action everyone was required to man the defences, rather than send running commentaries back home. As a result the radios on the German side often went quiet shortly after the commencement of action and progress had to be gleaned from the opposition. Although this was quite satisfactory in the vast majority of cases, it did not help when it came to serious action where the other side had enforced radio silence on its units. This meant many of the vitally important issues were missed until it was too late.

In any case, the German Navy hardly had the hardware in the Mediterranean to respond to powerful Allied threats and could not have done much to prevent the major events, such as the landings in southern Italy in 1943. From then on, it became very much a case of the German land forces retreating in an orderly fashion, rather than making an effort to turn back the Allied advance. Small units made desperate attempts to slow the advance, with bitter battles between German torpedo boats and the Royal Navy being fought among the small Greek islands into 1945 but generally it was more a case of the scorched earth policy, where considerable efforts were made to destroy any installation which might be of use to the Allies. It was evident from radio intercepts of Allied transmissions that there were a vast number of German pockets of resistance. Many of these managed to retreat to Germany, some became prisoners of war, but a good number vanished without leaving any evidence in the airwaves.

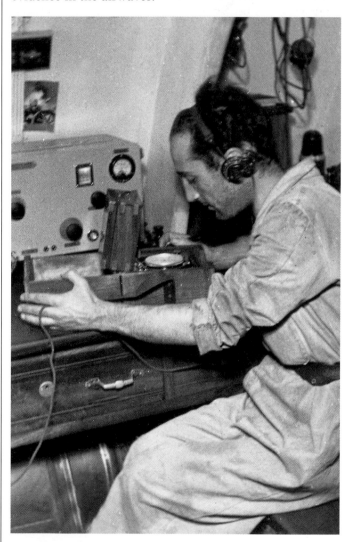

Above: The radio room of an Italian submarine. Although the majority of Italian boats were a good deal bigger than many of their German counterparts, the facilities on board were still exceedingly cramped and there was not much space to move around.

Chapter 12
Coastal Command, Normandy, D–Day and Thereafter

Coastal Command of the Royal Air Force started flying intensive patrols over the North Sea right from the beginning of the war. Many of these appeared to have been reconnaissance or training flights, and very few of them led to aggressive action. In addition, the Royal Navy's Fleet Air Arm was also flying anti-submarine patrols off aircraft carriers to the west of Britain, but these were stopped when the carrier HMS *Courageous* was sunk on 17 September 1939 by *U29* (Kptlt Otto Schuhart). The problem as far as the Radio Monitoring Service was concerned was that the RAF and carrier-based aircraft used their radios sparingly, only employing them when they had sighted something, which made the interception of messages rather tricky. This meant there was no way of predicting where and when aircraft were likely to appear, and all the information from the B-Dienst could be used for was to provide a running commentary of what the opposition was reporting. This, however, was quite useful, especially as many of U-boat commanders did not always see an aircraft attack as being a reason for radioing home in areas where aircraft were expected.

Extracting background information from the airwaves about the organisation of Coastal Command was not difficult and it was not long before Germany had a list of bases with details of the squadrons stationed there. Heinz Bonatz does not mention how this was done, but he did say that the majority of reports from aircraft included their squadron number as well as the identification of the individual plane. Some confusion was created by several groups using the same airfield, but generally it was possible to build up a picture of the land-based back up. It also became evident rather quickly that many of the new aircrew were fresh from school or an office job. The men might have been keen to volunteer, but they had little knowledge of the sea and the essential task of identifying targets was not easy. Very often the positions they sent did not correlate with the data collected by the radio direction finders and small destroyers were too often classed as huge battleships.

As the war progressed, the ever-increasing exchange of spoken messages around convoys and in the Bay of Biscay, where large numbers of Allied aircraft were active, was monitored in Germany and a special research programme was initiated to discover what was being said, the procedures being used and the type of equipment needed to cope with the most modern advances in radio techniques. Since the majority of these signals were not strong enough to reach land, all Germany could do was to send special research units into the hot spots. Finding men for such tasks was not easy. There were not many fluent English speakers with a knowledge of naval jargon and who were capable of distinguishing this from crackling and hissing radio sets. In any case, the general outcome of having such parties on board U-boats was not terribly helpful for solving the problems of the moment. The information gathered may have helped the B-Dienst in constructing the overall picture, but was less immediately helpful for finding a target or attacking it. The first of these

Above: Some of the radio staff aboard the auxiliary cruiser *Widder* under KptzS Hellmuth Ruckteschell, with the radio officer Dr Joachim Kindler holding the rather large microphone at the back.

Above: The badge on his left arm of this man indicates that he is a yeoman or clerk serving in Bordeaux in 1942. Many jobs with the B-Dienst were boring, mundane and repetitive, and thousands were employed to do nothing more than copy, sort and file papers. Yet this was such a vital part of the code-breaking process that the B-Dienst could not have functioned without such a vast army of dedicated workers.

listening parties had a definite exploratory function with a view to perhaps improving U-boat performance. All this changed quite rapidly throughout the latter part of 1943, when knowledge of what the enemy was doing was becoming more than a necessity as improvements in Allied anti-U-boat measures meant that it became increasingly difficult for the U-boats to avoid enemy aircraft and ships, and the attacks were becoming longer and more determined. This coincided with a more intensive Allied use of radar, and another desperate effort was made to find out what types of radio equipment the Allies were using and how knowledge of this could swing the war back into the German favour.

Radar became the chief suspect as the cause for the U-boats' demise as the Germans did not believe that the Enigma code had been compromised, in spite of the fact that the British and Americans seemed to have accurate knowledge of U-boat movements.

Sadly for Germany, the part of the listening research programme started towards the end of 1943 suffered a series of unfortunate setbacks. The radio expert, Dr Karl Greven, and his team of assistants set their gear up inside the already cramped quarters of *U406* (Kptlt Horst Dieterichs) with a view to leaving St Nazaire on 5 January 1944 to observe broadcasting activity in the Bay of Biscay. All this did was to provide the opposition with a reasonable insight into the state of German radio technology because the radio experts were among the survivors when *U406* was sunk on 18 January by the frigate *Spey* (Cdr H. G. Boys-Smith). A second team did not fare any better. It left Lorient aboard *U473* (Kptlt Heinz Sternberg) on 27 April, to be sunk a week later by the British sloops *Starling* (Cpt F. J. Walker), *Wild Goose* (Lt-Cdr R. W. Trethewey) and *Wren* (Lt-Cdr S. R. Woods).

Although the Allies landed in southern Italy on 3 September 1943, Germany suspected that such a spearhead could not sustain a thrust through Europe and another invasion, with a more direct supply route, was likely to follow. However, finding positive evidence for the location of such a move was not easy and therefore Germany prepared for every possible eventuality. Numerous war games were conducted to establish what was most likely to happen, each of which was based on the fundamental principle that any such landing had to be thrown back into the sea before it could gain a foothold on land. One of the main keys for solving this problem lay in knowing what forces the Allies had at their disposal and how this mass could be flung at continental Europe. Although good weather often allowed the Luftwaffe to fly reconnaissance sorties along the Channel ports, RAF superiority made it virtually impossible to proceed very far inland. Therefore, radio intelligence had to play a major role in extracting any useful clues of the anticipated landings.

The Supreme Command of all the German Armed Forces was under the impression the main thrust of the big invasion was likely to come in the Calais and Boulogne areas, where the Channel is the narrowest. Considerable research was made into the phases of the moon, tides and currents to see if it was possible to forecast some likely dates. However, the vast choice of possible options led to an abandonment of this line of research. The Navy was the junior partner in much of the defensive planning carried out by German High Command, although the preferred route, mentioned above, was least favoured from the nautical point of view. Many high ranking naval officers thought that the harbours of Dover and Folkestone were too small to accommodate an invasion fleet of hundreds of vessels, that the tidal conditions along the Pas de Calais were not advantageous for landings and that the currents were highly unsuitable for the type of craft needed to be got across the water. In addition, German defences had a number of heavy calibre guns along this part of the shore. The Navy also pointed out how the towns of Dover and Folkestone blocked access to their ports, making it a logistical headache for the Allies to bring the necessary vast volumes of materials and men into the harbours for boarding ships. Yet, despite the divergence in thinking, the admirals did agree that early summer of 1944 was a likely time for such an invasion.

One interesting point to emerge from naval radio intercept and direction finder stations was that the Supreme Command's estimates of the Allied build-up were rather high and it looked as if many units were being counted twice, but even something as simple as this was difficult to prove. Radio deception had become a daily occurrence and the intelligence officers spent considerable time and effort in sorting the obviously misleading information from reality. A steady build-up of troops in Kent in the southeast part of England — part of Allied deception — had already been established by the Supreme Command of the Armed Forces and aerial reconnaissance supported this with what appeared to be the signs of tank movements. In fact, the Allies had welded tank tracks around the outside of heavy rollers and towed these through obvious soft spots to scar the countryside with deep, tank-like ruts.

The B-Dienst's information did not fully agree with the build-up in Kent and it told the admirals there was an even more incriminating increase of shipping around Portsmouth, Poole and Weymouth. This was later confirmed by aerial reconnaissance photos. At the same time, the B-Dienst could not detect any significant movements further east. Dover, Folkestone, Newhaven and the Medway estuary, with the huge naval dockyard at Chatham, were almost deserted in comparison to the activity centred on Portsmouth. This discovery put the naval intercept stations on full alert to search for other incriminating evidence and it was not long before a

Intercepting messages involved taking down masses of jumbled letters and must have been one of the most boring of occupations, yet such a high level of concentration was required that the majority could keep it up for only brief periods. This highly demanding work could never have been tackled had there not been a mass of support staff who maintained and checked the equipment.

Above: This is an obviously posed picture showing typical telephonic equipment of the time on the wall.

Right: One of the younger members of the crew is seen relaying a concert being broadcast by radio to outside loudspeakers for men relaxing on the open deck of a patrol boat in 1942.

Right:
The British battleship *Ramillies* which was part of the naval force supporting 'Sword' beach during the Allied D-Day Normandy landings. *IAL*

Left:
Although severely outnumbered, German warships managed to make some attacks against Allied naval forces during the Normandy landings. Shown here is destroyer of the German 8th Destroyer Flotilla based in Brest during D-Day which attempted to break through into the Channel. *IAL*

Below:
The Royal Navy 'Tribal' class destroyer *Tartar* which was part of the British 10th Destroyer Flotilla which protected the western end of the Channel from enemy attack during the Normandy landings. She was severely damaged during an attack by German destroyers out of Brest. *IAL*

chain of unusual happenings was forthcoming. The BBC was broadcasting extraordinarily long radio messages to the French Resistance; night-time weather forecasts were being sent to United States aircraft, which were usually active only during the day; and German coastal radar stations along the Channel coast were being interfered with by ghost echoes. On top of this, long-running radio evidence of intensive training for amphibious landings on the Isle of Wight, in Dorset and in Devon stopped suddenly, shortly before D-Day. Much to the B-Dienst's surprise, this suggestive intelligence was disregarded by the Army and Air Force-dominated Supreme Command of the Armed Forces. Yet, despite this reticence, von Rundstedt, C-in-C West, the Commander of the Army in Normandy, did put his forces on alert shortly before the invasion, although there still were no direct indications in the airwaves of anything out of the ordinary being afoot which would affect that area.

The first clue for the B-Dienst in Berlin came shortly after dawn on 6 June with the intercept of an Allied signal which merely said, 'Details not yet available but we have landed.' It made the officers guess something was going on. However, there had been several earlier small-scale landings at St Nazaire, Dieppe and in other

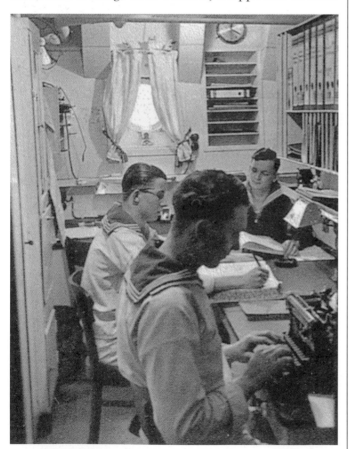

Above: Personnel working in land-based offices who complained about cramped conditions often had no idea about how hard things were for men aboard warships. The bull's-eye suggests that this shows a relatively spacious workplace on board a ship. On many smaller boats the radio cabin was too small to even stand up in.

places as well, so this could have been just another commando raid. It did not even say where the landing had taken place and there was no immediate response from the German side, but this was not unusual because the German intelligence officers tuned in to their own transmissions only when there was something serious afoot. On this occasion the heavily coded German messages continued to their addressees, rather than being intercepted and decoded. Bearing in mind the Allied signals had to be intercepted, passed on to decoders, translated, analysed and then sent on to the appropriate authority, it took some three hours before the B-Dienst sent a warning to the Supreme Naval Command, saying a large-scale landing could be imminent. The sour and obviously sarcastic answer told them it had already taken place and implied the interceptors were rather slow off the mark. The higher officers of the B-Dienst did not get unduly ruffled and pointed out that they had actually reported the presence of cross-Channel minesweeping activities during the night and that the Supreme Naval Command had been told there were special instructions also to clear shallow waters, which are not normally used by shipping. The B-Dienst had also forwarded a mass of other signals, but had hardly been kept informed of what was going on and therefore was working blind. In addition to this, it was pointed out how there had been a number of raids on radio intercept stations during the last two weeks, putting some totally out of action and severely curtailing the performance of others.

The names of the Normandy beaches, Sword, Omaha, Gold, Juno and Utah, have now become almost more famous than the real names and even feature on some atlases, but in 1944 it took a good while before the B-Dienst could work out what these meant. In addition to this, the British and American navies both started using new secret code systems. In Berlin, it was very much a case of looking awfully frustrated, making some strong ersatz coffee and puzzling the transmissions out. It took the best part of a week to gain some insight into this jumble of confusion and even when the messages started coming out in what looked like readable English, there were still enough disguised words to make interpretation difficult or even impossible. The whole issue was confusing enough for the B-Dienst not even to attempt working out the significance of some messages. However, this new code appeared to have been restricted to cross-Channel traffic. Other non-invasion transmitters as well as distress signals could still be read.

The B-Dienst was still recovering from the surprise and scale of the invasion when, despite the new radio codes, no less than 10 Allied anti-submarine support groups were identified along the western reaches of the Channel. Three or four of them appeared to be constantly on patrol, running across the sea as a continuous chain. In addition to this, the increased intensity of air patrols for

Above: Part of the land-based radio room at the 3rd U-boat Flotilla with the blackout curtain in position. This shows how radio operators worked under quite spartan conditions, often lacking the basic necessities taken for granted in so many private offices.

Operation 'Cork', to seal off the approaches to the invasion supply routes, did not go unnoticed by the B-Dienst. Despite this massive effort, all U-boats in the Biscay ports were ordered to be sent against the invasion traffic. This almost suicidal effort turned into a one-sided battle from which no U-boat returned unscathed and many were lost. Radio beacon signals from German monitoring stations played a vital part in getting the few survivors back home. Being constantly pushed under meant the majority of crews could not take accurate bearings on sun or stars, making navigation exceedingly tricky and errors of well over 200 kilometres were not unusual. To give just one example of these navigational problems: *U763* (Kptlt Ernst Cordes) became totally lost in early July 1944 as a result of long and exhausting chases. On sighting land, the radio operator took a bearing on the Brest transmitter, which suggested they were somewhere among the Channel Islands. Not long afterwards the men were horrified to discover they had accidentally drifted into the Royal Navy's anchorage at Spithead and could see the Portsmouth naval base through the periscope.

It took about a few days to gain an insight in the new D-Day radio code, but once this had been done it became possible to read intercepts at a relatively fast rate. The brains of the cryptanalysts were still spinning from the hard effort when they were rewarded with fascinating information. The senior officer of the Allied

Ferry Control sent daily reports to Britain, listing everything which had been landed during the preceding 24 hours. What is more, the same office obliged by adding up the totals and transmitting those towards the end of each week. This was useful, but the German Navy hardly had the resources to slow it down. However, this time the natural elements were on the German side. An unusually ferocious storm on 19 June destroyed the temporary harbours on the invasion beaches, although it also put paid to the regular reports of what was being brought across the Channel. The B-Dienst was kept busy with a flood of distress signals calling for help, while just as many ships gave away their positions by saying they had found relatively safe refuges in remote bays.

All this was still being digested when British reports of pilotless aircraft started flooding into Berlin. Of course, the B-Dienst was aware of the so-called revenge weapons and quickly gathered that the first V1 rockets, with their simple pulse jet engines, were on their way. They had a measuring device to shut off the fuel after a pre-adjusted distance and thus bring the bomb onto its target. Setting this for a small area such as the coastal towns added considerable problems to the difficult task

Above: This shows the accommodation blocks for the U-boat base in Bergen (Norway) and no doubt B-Dienst quarters would have been in similar types of buildings.

Above: Men from *U393* relaxing with their accommodation barrack in the background. This shows the type of rickety quarters used by the Navy, and many B-Dienst men would have been accommodated in similar buildings throughout the occupied countries.

of getting the adjustment right. The V1 was not aimed by allowing it simply to run out of fuel, as has often been suggested.

The V1 news from Britain was still being digested in Berlin when the B-Dienst was puzzled by reports of these proceeding under water. At first this was put down to highly imaginative thinking, but then the term 'One Man Torpedo' appeared in a decrypt, confirming that German midget submarines had arrived at the front. The B-Dienst knew such devices were on their way but had not known exactly what state of readiness they were in. However, the B-Dienst was left in doubt of the fear these instilled in some sectors of the opposition. A depth charge, even one very wide of its mark, was likely to put paid to a one-man submarine, but they were attacking in relatively confined waters among the invasion unloading areas, where it was impractical to hurl depth charges about. To make matters worse, even when not anchored, the majority of these ferries were too clumsy to be able to manoeuvre away from a highly agile midget submarine. The problem was quickly solved by the unloading process itself. Since the majority of harbour installations had been destroyed, many ships were being emptied in shallow water by landing craft and it was a simple matter of equipping one of them with five-pound bombs and allowing it to chug around the main target once attackers had been sighted. Although this sounds terribly amateurish, the improvisation did work. When more reports started flooding in, the B-Dienst was astonished to learn how many pilots-cum-operators were actually captured alive to be made prisoners of war. No doubt they were lucky to have got out of their uncomfortable coffins in time.

The Allied thrust to capture the port of Cherbourg apparently, from intercepts, went according to plan, but when they got there on 27 June, the Allies were most disappointed with the state of the harbour. Not only had the installations been destroyed, but wrecks made some quays unusable and a breach in the mole or breakwater allowed the full force of the Atlantic weather to blast the few available berths, making them not ideal places for unloading. The B-Dienst continued to pick up clues about the Allied advance east, as well as the move west

Above: The Supreme Naval Command in Berlin was bombed out during the middle of the war and vital offices had to be distributed around out-of-the-way locations where they could work undisturbed until bunkers like this one could be made available. This shows an average-sized command bunker at the Torpedo Trials Centre in Eckernförde, but similar buildings were constructed in and around the major western bases. A high proportion of them are still standing, although many are nowadays less conspicuous.

towards Brest (taken by the Allies on 21 September) and the possibility of the Channel Islands being retaken. (In the end, the Channel Islands were bypassed by the Allies, leaving the people there to endure another harsh winter with very little supplies getting through, before being retaken in 1945 at the end of the war.)

The B-Dienst was kept busier than ever before, following the Allied advance towards several key naval bases in France, but many of the expected high-intensity battles did not take place. Instead the Allied armies often avoided the hot spots, giving the cut-off troops in the ports the opportunity of surrendering or starving. Many radio stations, including B-Dienst bases, had to be abandoned and key personnel moved to other places. Those left operational were kept busy with day-to-day traffic and the usual distress calls, but the majority of these were caused by ships running aground or colliding, rather than by enemy action. Nobody expected great victories from the few midget weapons, E-boats, U-boats and other small craft employed along the continental coast, although some of them did achieve some striking results, attacking with great

tenacity and ingenuity. Even men from the German forces on the cut-off Channel Islands found the resources and energy to launch an attack against Granville (France) just one month before the end of the war. A small flotilla of scrounged-together remnants (four minesweepers, three gun carriers and six smaller vessels) left St Helier on Jersey shortly after nightfall on 8 March 1945 to be rewarded with the sinking of four coastal steamers in Granville harbour, the release of almost 70 prisoners of war and the capture of one collier in the commando raid. It was a sterling effort, but the pressing realities of the war in Germany meant that the B-Dienst was hardly capable of following such exploits. The Radio Monitoring system had shrunk to a tiny core, which was focused mainly on the Baltic, where Germany's biggest battle was being fought to evacuate over two million refugees from the east, to get them out of the clutches of the advancing Red Army.

The contracting eastern and western fronts resulted in the closure of many intercept and radio direction finding stations as well as the withdrawal of the highly specialised staff, which made it exceedingly difficult for

Above: Burning secret papers at Nordblitz naval camp in Norway on 8 May 1945, a few days after the Instrument of Surrender had been signed. The High Command took the view that the navy had nothing to hide and therefore records and log books were to be preserved. However, radio operators especially have the need for absolute secrecy instilled in them and they often destroyed sensitive operational material before the enemy could lay its hand on information which might compromise other units. The destruction of documents which might be useful to the enemy caused serious disruption during the hurried evacuation of some French bases and many people remained at their posts, risking capture, in order to burn papers.

the B-Dienst to participate in what was to become one of the biggest rescue operations in history, although the B-Dienst did keep tabs on the number of Russian naval forces in the Baltic and maintained a regular forecast of available aircraft. However, the situation at the front was so chaotic and the times between obtaining the information and having to act upon it so short that much of this work went by the wayside. In addition, tracing the B-Dienst's activities during this time is made more difficult by the fact that the majority of records were burned after evaluation as life in the various radio monitoring centres had become so hectic. There was just no longer any staff to classify and to store the documents. Germany's eastern frontier was pushed westwards at such an alarmingly fast rate that it was very difficult for the intelligence services to keep track of what was going on. Very often it was a case of reversed effort, where commanders at the front were updating intelligence officers, rather than the other way round. The German Navy assisted in evacuating well over two million people from the Baltic regions under desperately cold conditions, over vast distances of several hundred miles and under the most painfully chaotic circumstances but if the B-Dienst did make any significant inroads in helping this mass of humanity, records of those achievements were not preserved in the chaos.

Much of the B-Dienst activity came to a crashing halt long before the end of the war. Homes, offices and other workplaces were destroyed to such an extent that there were no longer any facilities for continuing much of its operations. In addition to this, the communication network was severely disrupted, often making it impossible to establish contact with out stations or to pass on vital information. Many of the naval headquarters became so disorganised towards the end of the war that there were times when the B-Dienst did not even know where the appropriate headquarters had been relocated to. These photographs of Lorient (*above*) and Heligoland (*opposite*) show the condition of many buildings in the naval bases by the end of the war, where working conditions became increasingly difficult.

Above: This picture, taken in Kiel during the early months of 2001, shows the type of bunker used to accommodate naval offices towards the end of the war. Similar buildings were hastily erected in many of the main centres to protect vital centres and, towards the end of the war, the B-Dienst operated in a similar structure near Berlin.

Below: The Flandernbunker in Kiel. It appears that there was some large valuable machinery inside, which could be removed only by cutting large holes into the massive walls.

Anatomy of a World War 2 Radio Station

The following photographs of the radio transmitting station at Kingstanding in Ashdown Forest have been included to give some idea of what World War 2 radio stations would have looked like. German radio stations still standing at the end of the war were demolished by the Allies and very little of them remains to give any impression of these enormous installations. The radio transmitters at Kingstanding housed 'Aspidistra', then the world's most powerful radio transmitter, which was used for sending black propaganda programmes to Germany. Although this has no direct connection with the radio stations used for transmitting naval signals, it does show the size and layout of such installations, and gives an indication of what a radio station of the period looked like.

The photographs of the remains of the radio station were taken with the kind permission of the West Sussex Police and we are most grateful to Terry Beckwith for all his help and encouragement.

Above: The entrance to what had been 'Aspidistra', Britain's black radio station which transmitted to Germany throughout much of World War 2. Tank obstacles can be seen on both sides of the drive. It is located in the Ashdown Forest, by the side of the B2026 road running between Hartfield and Maresfield. This photograph was taken in 2001, long after the station had been closed. Some information about this interesting radio transmitter can be found at Bletchley Park in Milton Keynes (Buckinghamshire), home of the British code breakers during the war and now a museum.

Right: The last remaining radio mast at 'Aspidistra' in Ashdown Forest. During the war there were three much bigger masts here, presenting a spider's web of lines strung over tall pylon-like towers. This small mast marks the spot where several 100m-high (300ft) aerials stood during the war.

Below left: The aerial switching house, showing the insulators built into the wall. Changing the power supply to the various aerials was a precision job and was carried out from this circular building at the old 'Aspidistra' site.

Below right: Old wartime buildings can sometimes be identified by the presence of a blast protection wall, which can be seen here in front of the doors towards the right.

Left: The so-called 'Cinema' at Kingstanding which used to house the transmitters for broadcasting the black propaganda channel, *Soldatensender Calais und Atlantik*.

Below left: The main entrance of the bunker housing the world's most powerful radio transmitter at the time, code-named 'Aspidistra', after the song made famous by Gracie Fields. This doorway is now used only as an emergency exit. During the war the entrance looked much plusher and even had fish tanks incorporated into the wall. The main 'Aspidistra' bunker was converted into an atomic shelter after the war.

Below right: The entrance to the main underground radio station at Kingstanding in Ashdown Forest. Digging this massive 50ft (15m) deep hole was a tremendous undertaking in itself and building the concrete bunker with a roof several feet thick was not easy. The construction was made more difficult by exceptionally cold winter weather, which meant fires had to be kept burning around the site to prevent men, machinery and soft concrete from freezing solid.

Further Reading

Beesly, Patrick; *Very Special Intelligence*; Hamish Hamilton, London, 1977 and Doubleday, New York, 1978. (An interesting book dealing with the Operational Intelligence Centre in London by the deputy leader of the Submarine Tracking Room.)

Bonatz, Heinz; *Seekrieg im Äther*; Mittler & Sohn, Herford, 1981. (The author was the Head of the B-Dienst for much of the war and in this book he has presented a most comprehensive account of the Radio Monitoring Service, but it must rank as one of the most difficult to read due to the many abbreviations, some of them without explanation.)

Die Deutsche Marine-Funkaufklärung 1914–1945; Wehr und Wissen, Darmstadt, 1970

Busch, Harald; *So war der Ubootskrieg* (*U-boats at War*); Deutsche Heimat Verlag, Bielefeld, 1954. (This early account by an ex-war-correspondent has become a classic on this subject.)

Dönitz, Karl; *Ten Years and Twenty Days*; Weidenfeld and Nicolson, London, 1959.

Mein wechselvolles Leben; Musterschmidt Verlag, Frankfurt, 1968.

Frank, Wolfgang; *Die Wölfe und der Admiral*; Gerhard Stalling Verlag, Oldenburg, 1953. Translated as *Sea Wolves — The Story of the German U-boat War*; Weidenfeld, London, 1955. (An excellent classic written by a war correspondent who served aboard U-boats.)

Gellermann, Günther W.; *Und lauschten für Hitler*; Bernard & Graefe Verlag, Bonn, 1991. (An interesting book dealing with the non-naval side of the German Radio Monitoring Service.)

Tief im Hinterland des Gegners; Bernard & Graefe Verlag, Bonn, 1999.

Giese, Otto and Wise, Capt. James E.; *Shooting the War*; Naval Institute Press, Annapolis, 1994. (A fascinating book. Giese ran the blockade aboard the merchant ship *Anneliese Essberger* and then joined the U-boat arm to serve in the Arctic, Atlantic and Far East.)

Giessler, Helmuth; *Der Marine-Nachrichten-und-Ortungsdienst*, J.F. Lehmanns Verlag, Munich, 1971.

Gretton, Sir Peter; *Convoy Escort Commander*; Cassell, London, 1964.

Gröner, Erich; *Die Handelsflotten der Welt 1942*; J.F. Lehmanns, Munich, reprinted 1976. (Includes details of ships sunk up to 1942. This valuable publication was originally a confidential document and contains a complete list of ships, in similar style to Lloyd's Register. There is also a lengthy section with good line drawings.)

Herzog, Bodo; *60 Jahre deutsche U-boote 1906-1966*; J.F. Lehmanns, Munich, 1968. (A useful book with much tabulated information.)

U-boats in Action; Ian Allan Publishing, Shepperton, and Podzun, Dorheim. (A pictorial book with captions in English.)

Hessler, Günter, Hoschatt, Alfred and others; *The U-boat War in the Atlantic*; HMSO, 1989.

Hirschfeld, Wolfgang; *Feindfahrten*; Neff, Vienna, 1982. (The secret diary of a U-boat radio operator compiled in the radio rooms of operational submarines. A most invaluable insight into the war and probably one of the most significant accounts of the war at sea.)

Das Letzte Boot — Atlantik Farewell; Universitas, Munich, 1989. (The last journey of U234, surrender in the United States and life as a prisoner of war.)

Hirschfeld, Wolfgang and Brooks Geoffrey; *Hirschfeld — The Story of a U-boat NCO 1940-46*; Leo Cooper, London, 1996. (A fascinating English language edition of Hirschfeld's life in U-boats.)

Kohnen, David; *Commanders Winn and Knowles: Winning the U-boat War with Intelligence 1939-1943*; The Enigma Press, Krakow, 1999. (An interesting book, although the name Rodger Winn is misspelled as Roger throughout.)

Lohmann, W. and Hildebrand, H. H.; *Die deutsche Kriegsmarine 1939–1945*; Podzun, Dorheim, 1956–1964. (This multi-volume work is the standard reference document on the German Navy, giving details of ships, organisation and personnel.)

Macintyre, Donald; *The Battle of the Atlantic*; Batsford, London, 1971.

Möller, Eberhard; *Kurs Atlantik*; Motorbuch Verlag, Stuttgart, 1995.

Moore, Captain Arthur R.; *A careless word... a needless sinking*; American Merchant Marine Museum, Maine, 1983. (A detailed and well-illustrated account of ships lost during the war.)

OKM; *Rangliste der deutschen Kriegsmarine*; Mittler & Sohn, published annually, Berlin.

Handbuch für U-boot-Kommandanten; Berlin, 1942. Translated during the war and published by Thomas Publications, Gettysburg, 1989 as *The U-boat Commander's Handbook*.

Raeder, Erich; *Struggle for the Sea*; William Kimber, London, 1966.

My Life; US Naval Institute Press, 1960.

Rohwer, J.; *Axis Submarine Successes of World War II 1939–45*; Greenhill, London, 1998.

The Critical Convoy Battles of March 1943; Ian Allan Publishing, London, 1977.

Rohwer, J. and Hümmelchen, G.; *Chronology of the War at Sea 1939–1945*; Greenhill, London, 1992. (A good, solid and informative work. Well indexed and most useful for anyone studying the war at sea.)

Rohwer, J. and Jäckel, Eberhard; *Die Funkaufklärung und ihre Rolle im 2. Weltkrieg*; Motorbuch Verlag, Stuttgart, 1979. (An interesting collection of lectures presented at a conference in Bad Godesberg (Bonn) by a variety of contributors.)

Rohwer, J. and Jacobsen, H.A.; *Decisive Battles of World War II*; A. Deutsch, London, 1965.

Roskill, Captain S. W.; *The War at Sea*; 4 vols, HMSO, London, 1954, reprinted 1976. (The British official history of the war at sea.)

Schlemm, Jürgen; *Der U-Boot-Krieg 1939–1945 in der Literatur*; Elbe-Spree-Verlag, Hamburg and Berlin, 2000. (A comprehensive bibliography of publications about the U-boat war.)

Schoenfeld, Max; *Stalking the U-boat*; Smithsonian Institution Press, Washington and London, 1995. (An interesting account about the USAAF's offensive anti-submarine operations.)

Sharpe, Peter; *U-boat Fact File*; Midland Publishing, Leicester, 1998. (A handy reference book, well laid out and easy to use.)

Showell, Jak P. Mallmann; *The German Navy in World War Two*; Arms and Armour Press, London, 1979; Naval Institute Press, Annapolis 1979 and translated as *Das Buch der deutschen Kriegsmarine*, Motorbuch Verlag, Stuttgart, 1982. (Covers history, organisation, the ships, code writers, naval charts and a section on ranks, uniforms, awards and insignias by Gordon Williamson. Named by the United States Naval Institute as 'One of the Outstanding Naval Books of the Year'.)

U-boats under the Swastika; Ian Allan Publishing, Shepperton, 1973; Arco, New York, 1973 and translated as *Uboote gegen England*, Motorbuch, Stuttgart, 1974. (A well-illustrated introduction to the German U-boat Arm, which is now one of the longest selling naval books in Germany.)

U-boats under the Swastika; Ian Allan Publishing, London, 1987. (A second edition of the above title with different photos and new text.)

U-boat Command and the Battle of the Atlantic; Conway Maritime Press, London, 1989; Vanwell, New York, 1989. (A detailed history based on the U-boat Command's war diary.)

Germania International; Journal of the German Navy Study Group. Now out of print.

U-boat Commanders and Crews; The Crowood Press, Marlborough, 1998. Translated as *Die U-Boot-Waffe: Kommandanten und Besatzungen*; Motorbuch Verlag, Stuttgart, 2001.

German Navy Handbook 1939–1945; Sutton Publishing, Stroud, 1999. Translated as *Kriegsmarine 1939-1945*; Motorbuch Verlag, Stuttgart, 2000.

U-boats in Camera 1939–1945; Sutton Publishing, Stroud, 1999.

Enigma U-boats, Ian Allan Publishing, London 2000.

U-boats at War — Landings on Hostile Shores; Ian Allan Publishing, London, 2000.

Atlantic U-boat Bunkers; Sutton Publishing, Stroud, 2001.

What Britain Knew and Wanted to Know about U-boats, selected, annotated reprints from the secret Monthly Anti-Submarine Reports; published for U-Boot-Archiv by Military Press, Milton Keynes, 2001.

Weapons used against U-boats; selected reprints from the secret Monthly Anti-Submarine Reports; published for U-boot-Archiv by Military Press, Milton Keynes, 2002.

Smith, Constance Babington; *Evidence in Camera*; David & Charles, Newton Abbot, 1957 and 1974. (An interesting book about British aerial photo reconnaissance.)

U-Boot-Archiv; *Das Archiv* (German) *The U-boat Archive* (English language); a journal published twice a year for members of FTU, U-Boot-Archiv, Bahnhofstrasse 57, D27478 Cuxhaven-Altenbruch. (Please enclose at least two International Postal Reply Coupons if asking for details.)

Ulsamer, Gregor; *Feuerschiff Borkumriff*; VDE Verlag, Berlin and Offenbach, 1997. (A fascinating history of the coastal radio stations on the Island of Borkum.)

Verband Deutscher Ubootsfahrer; *Schaltung Küste*; (Journal of the German Submariners' Association)

Wagner, Gerhard (editor); *Lagevorträge des Oberbefehlshabers der Kriegsmarine vor Hitler*; J. F. Lehmanns, Munich, 1972. Translated as *Führer Conferences on Naval Affairs*, Greenhill, London, reprinted with new introduction 1990. (The first English language edition was published before the German version.)

Winterbotham, F.W.; *The Ultra Secret*; Purnell Book Services, London, 1974.

Witthöft, Hans Jürgen; *Lexikon zur deutschen Marinegeschichte*; Koehler, Herford, 1977. (An excellent two-volume encyclopaedia.)

Wynn, Kenneth; *U-boat Operations of the Second World War*; Chatham, London, 1997.

The main entrance to the Federal Military complex at Nordholz, near Cuxhaven, which housed one of the first coastal radio stations. The site at Nordholz is still used by the military to this day day and there are numerous notices telling uninvited visitors that they are not welcome. The World War 2 masts holding up the aerials for the coastal radio station at Nordholz were located in an area of heather and low scrubland, some distance behind the main entrance. These structures were demolished by the Allies shortly after the end of the war and the land was planted with firs and pines.

The Organisation of the Naval Intelligence Service

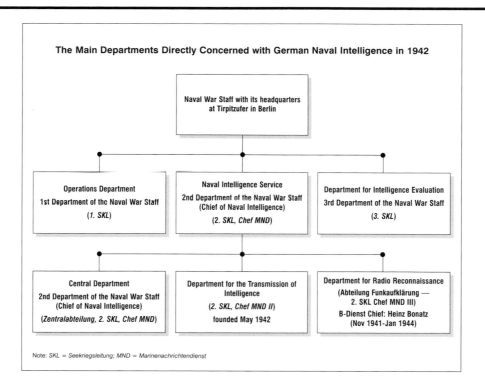

The Main Departments Directly Concerned with German Naval Intelligence in 1942

Naval War Staff with its headquarters at Tirpitzufer in Berlin

Operations Department
1st Department of the Naval War Staff
(1. SKL)

Naval Intelligence Service
2nd Department of the Naval War Staff
(Chief of Naval Intelligence)
(2. SKL, Chef MND)

Department for Intelligence Evaluation
3rd Department of the Naval War Staff
(3. SKL)

Central Department
2nd Department of the Naval War Staff
(Chief of Naval Intelligence)
(Zentralabteilung, 2. SKL, Chef MND)

Department for the Transmission of Intelligence
(2. SKL, Chef MND II)
founded May 1942

Department for Radio Reconnaissance
(Abteilung Funkaufklärung —
2. SKL Chef MND III)
B-Dienst Chief: Heinz Bonatz
(Nov 1941-Jan 1944)

Note: SKL = Seekriegsleitung; MND = Marinenachrichtendienst

October 1934

Six months before the new defence laws were introduced and the so-called Treaty of Versailles was repudiated by Hitler, a Naval Intelligence Department was created by amalgamating the three older information-gathering organisations: Foreign Navies, Intelligence Distribution and Radio Reconnaissance. The Departmental Head was KS Theodor Arps, who remained in office until December 1939.

January 1940

The Naval Intelligence Department was reorganised to occupy a more central role within the Supreme Naval Command and KS Ludwig Stummel became head until June 1941.

June 1941

So far, intelligence gathering and assimilation had been controlled by the Naval Intelligence Inspectorate (Marinenachrichteninspektion) and this was upgraded in June 1941 to become the Naval Intelligence Service (Marinenachrichtendienst).

Commanding Officers of the Naval Intelligence Service

Jun 41–May 43   VA Erhard Maertens
May 43–Aug 44   KA Ludwig Stummel
Aug 44–End war   KA Fritz Krauss

Central Department

(Created in June 1941 and reduced considerably in size during September 1944)
Departmental Heads:
Jun 41–May 43   KS Ludwig Stummel
May 43–Sep 44   KS Fritz Krauss

Department for the Transmission of Intelligence

(Created as an autonomous department in May 1942)
Departmental Heads:
May 42–May 43   KS Hans Möller
May 43–Jan 44   KS Max Kupfer
Jan 44–End   KS Henno Lucan

Radio Reconnaissance Department (B-Dienst)

(Created as an autonomous department in November 1941)
Departmental Heads:
Nov 41–Jan 44   KS Heinz Bonatz
Jan 44–End   KS Max Kupfer

In addition to the above, there were also departments dealing with radar evaluation, radio direction finding and land-line communications, but these were only operational for a period of a few months and were somewhat divorced from the main intelligence gathering organisations.

KS = Kapitän zur See; KA = Konteradmiral, VA = Vizeadmiral

Appendix II
The Radio Monitoring Service Stations

At the Beginning of World War 2

Some of the radio stations were located in tiny villages which are exceedingly difficult to identify and to find in modern atlases. They have therefore been omitted from this list.

Headquarters:	Berlin
North Sea Coastal Radio Chain:	Wilhelmshaven, Borkum, List, Nordholz
Baltic Coastal Radio Chain:	Kiel, Neumünster, Falshöft, Cape Arkona, Swinemünde, Stolpmünde, Pillau
Inland Radio Stations:	Soest, Langenargen (Lake Constance), Neusiedl-am-See (Austria), Landsberg

The Radio Monitoring Service During the War

Baltic:	As above but with more temporary stations further east for a brief period in 1941–3; Reval
German Bight:	As above
Germany Inland:	As above
Flanders:	Groningen, Den Helder, Hoek van Holland, Brugge (later Brussels), Boulogne, Dieppe, Fécamp, Etretat.
West France:	Brest, Angers, Bayeux, Erquy
S.W. France:	Bordeaux
Norway:	Kirkenes, Hammerfest, Tromsö, Harstad, Narvik, Bodö, Mo, Mosjoen, Namsos, Trondheim, Kristiansund, Alesund, Bergen, Stavanger, Kristiansand, Oslo.
Denmark:	Hjörring
Mediterranean:	Madrid and Seville in Spain; Montpellier and Toulon in France; Carrara, Genzano di Roma, Padua and Nervi in Italy; Athens and Loutza in Greece; Sicily.
Black Sea:	Constanta, Burgas and Feodosiya.

Most of the major centres also supervised a number of out-stations in their vicinity.

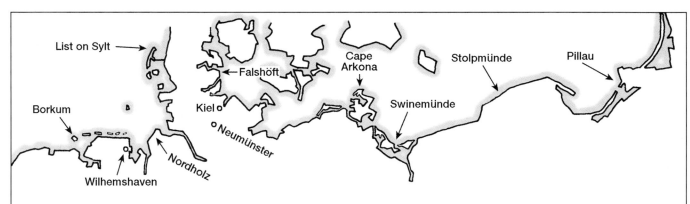

The Coastal Chain of Radio Direction Finder and Intercept Stations at the Start of the War

Further South were: Langenargen on Lake Constance and Neusiedl am See

Daily Contributions from the Radio Monitoring Service

Intercepted signals, whether decoded or not, were evaluated, sorted according to the type of message it was likely to be and quickly passed on to the appropriate authorities for immediate action. Much of this information then vanished into official incinerators. The majority of operational commanders neither had the staff nor the facilities for storing it, although some of the major news items were mentioned in their war diaries. The Intelligence Service did classify and keep many of the original intercepts, but, unlike Britain, did not maintain such a vast intelligence backup service. The operational urgent messages were stripped of their routine clutter and confusing abbreviations to make it easier for higher commanders to comprehend and this news was then passed up the chain of command to the Operations Department and to the Naval War Staff or Supreme Naval Command. By the time it reached the Supreme Naval Command, the intercepted news usually contained only the basic essence and individual commanders had to ask if they wanted more information. Yet, although only the basic essence was stored, the material still filled several A4 folders for each month of the war. Heinz Bonatz, as Head of MND III — the German Naval Intelligence Department for Radio Reconnaissance (the B-Dienst), also issued a weekly summary of the findings of the German Naval Radio Monitoring Service to the Supreme Naval Command. These were called X-B Bulletins.

The following is an example of the daily reports for a period of about 40 days, chosen at random, to illustrate the type of information which was supplied by the intelligence services to the Supreme Naval Command. It has been rewritten for modern readers who do not necessarily have the background knowledge which the admirals would have had. On top of this, much of the repetition is omitted. The usual mishmash of naval abbreviation has also been left out. Hopefully, this will provide some understanding of the type of material contributed by the Radio Monitoring Service throughout the war to the Chiefs of the Naval War Staff.

The words 'English' and 'British' have been kept as they were used in the original and nm stands for nautical miles (*Seemeilen* in German).

This extract comes from the *Kriegstagebuch der Seekriegsleitung*. This work has been reprinted and published by Mittler und Sohn in 64 volumes, copies of which can be found in U-Boot-Archiv.

1939

27 December
Towards evening, the cruiser *Sheffield* was some 150nm west of Jutland. Earlier the B-Dienst discovered three or four destroyers in this area and one was found by air reconnaissance. A submarine was detected 40nm northwest of Skagen (the northern tip of Denmark).

An agent has reported a heavy cruiser has arrived in Devonport during the middle of December for repairs.

31 December
According to Daventry radio, the authorities in Montevideo have ordered the master of the German freighter *Tacoma* to leave within 24 hours, otherwise the ship will be interned.

Above: The German freighter *Tacoma* in wartime camouflage. *IAL*

1940

19 July

The Royal Air Force is being reorganised to respond more quickly to any attempted landing on the English south coast. German bases in Holland, Belgium and France have been given high priority for bomber targets and every effort is to be made to reconnoitre areas where German ships or barges are likely to assemble.

Aircraft carrier *Argus* is in the Clyde area. Cruiser *Vindictive* has left Devonport in a westerly direction. Cruiser *Australia* is on her way to the Clyde. Auxiliary cruiser *Laurentic* is near Iceland and *Voltaire* is covering convoy HX59 from Halifax to England. Cruiser *Caradoc* is heading east; at present about 300nm east of Halifax. Cruiser *Bonaventure* is about 350nm east of Halifax.

27 August

English merchant ships and fishing boats have been given orders to attack all enemy aircraft which come within range of their guns. Therefore, English aircraft have been told keep at least 1,400 metres away from ships at sea. There is evidence from radio intercepts that special anti-air raid precautions are being taken in the English and Bristol Channel areas. Details of enemy dispositions in other sea areas are not available at the moment.

14 September

Central Atlantic: Spanish reports state there are a number of English destroyers around the Cape Verde Islands and these could be connected with convoys to Freetown in Africa, which are using the islands for emergency anchorages when they need to avoid our forces.

Active radio communications between Task Force H and the Commander-in-Chief for the South Atlantic suggests there are some joint operations with the task force off Freetown (*Dorsetshire*, *Delhi*, *Vindictive* and *Albatross*). Italian radio direction finders have located *Renown* 30nm southwest of Cape Spartel, the northern tip of Africa opposite Gibraltar. A battleship and several destroyers have been reported to be off Tangiers in Morocco.

It has been impossible to provide details of the task force in the Atlantic, but we do know that *Ark Royal*, together with supporting cruisers and destroyers, is still at sea.

Italian sources have reported an aircraft carrier, probably *Hermes*, with the cruiser *Dragon* off Aden in the Indian Ocean. They have escorted convoy RS5 (Gibraltar to Freetown).

A new minefield has been identified in the North Sea and is visible from the air as a number of oily patches in the water. It would seem that this has been laid to hinder a German invasion of Britain from Norway.

29 September

Radio direction finders have discovered unidentified formations to the west of the Shetland Isles and north of Ireland. They are some 300nm west and 80-100nm north of Ireland.

Battleship *Renown*, together with destroyer escort, arrived at Gibraltar yesterday and is due to leave again early tomorrow. A French task force commander and destroyers are heading west which suggests some special mission is under way. Weather conditions in the area are favourable for such an undertaking. Spanish connections tell us there is lively traffic heading towards England.

Last night saw particularly meticulous patrols along the English southeast coast, especially around Great Yarmouth. There were seven larger ships, 18 minesweepers, four submarine chasers and 48 patrol boats. Forty-three of these patrol units were identified around the Yarmouth–Harwich area. All this points to forces around the Dover area being put on high alert.

An enemy submarine has been spotted 60nm off Terschelling (Holland) and there are active convoy movements along England's east coast. There are 12 destroyers in Harwich and another six at sea further east. A convoy of 50 medium-sized ships has been detected northeast of Southend, heading towards the Thames.

1 October

Various convoys have been detected northwest of Ireland, in the Irish Sea and 300nm west of southern Ireland. Two British auxiliary cruisers and other forces have been located west of South Africa.

Very few ships and correspondingly little radio traffic have been detected along the English south coast. There is a convoy with destroyer escorts in the Pentland Firth and more convoys further south along the English east coast. Air reconnaissance photos show the battleships *Rodney* and *Nelson* together with several destroyers anchored in Firth of Forth.

2 October

Reports from English aircraft have given an insight into convoy procedures. An eastbound convoy has been located near Ireland. The 2,300grt freighter *D. Latymer* has run into difficulties southwest of Ireland after receiving some bomb hits.

News of English shipping close to the Spanish coast has been confirmed by reports from Spain. One unidentified submarine is known to be off Cape Finisterre (Spain).

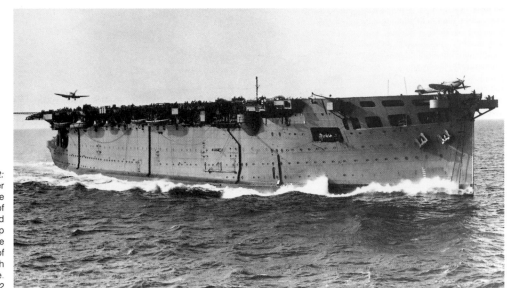

Right:
The British aircraft carrier *Argus*, seen here operating off the coast of North Africa. Converted from a merchant ship during World War 1, she survived until the end of World War 2, although latterly in reserve. *IWM AI2882*

Left:
The Royal Navy 'Norfolk' class cruiser *Dorsetshire*, sunk in the Pacific in 1942 by Japanese aircraft. *IAL*

Right:
Royal Navy aircraft carrier HMS *Ark Royal* was launched in 1937 and had quickly amassed an impressive service history in the Atlantic and Mediterranean, including her Swordfish aircraft being involved in the sinking of the *Bismarck*, before she was torpedoed and sunk by *U81* in the western Mediterranean in November 1941. *IAL*

Above: HMS *Renown*, the British battlecruiser dating from World War 1 which served throughout World War 2. *IAL*

There is a group of English battleships off Freetown, probably moving northwards.

Patrols and minesweeping activities in the North Sea have become very lively again. Four bigger ships and 88 other vessels have been identified. Seventy-seven of these are in the Great Yarmouth–Harwich area. There are 10 fleet units and 16 escorts in the Thames estuary. Two ships were found by radio location methods to be near Dogger Bank in the North Sea.

Air reconnaissance has confirmed there is lively shipping traffic along England's east and south coasts. Twenty ships with four destroyers are heading south near Orford Ness (north of Harwich), there is a cruiser near Southend, a tanker with a destroyer near Ramsgate, three destroyers near Grimsby and there is also lively traffic in the Thames estuary. Fifty to 60 merchant ships and numerous smaller ships have been located between the Firth of Forth and Aberdeen.

Warships faithful to General de Gaulle, namely *De Brassa*, *Duboo* and *Domine*, have been sighted along the Ivory Coast. Bougainville informed the submarine *Poncelet* that de Gaulle's flotilla is probably going to Gabon.

3 October
The majority of the people living on Malta would like to see an end to the war. Numerous sources have revealed unrest is increasing considerably, especially in view of the highly inadequate air raid provisions for civilians and the unbearable living conditions for the majority of ordinary people.

Various convoys and other shipping movements have been detected in the Irish Sea and around the North Channel through radio intercepts from enemy aircraft. One position has been determined from an enemy submarine warning, telling various ships how to avoid it.

There are still active patrols along the English east and south coasts, together with several convoys, especially in the Thames Estuary. An enemy submarine has been located off Terschelling Bank (Holland). Radio direction finders have located a larger ship some 10nm west of Calais and there is an English submarine near Cap Gris Nez. This has been confirmed by our 4th Minesweeping Flotilla.

4 October

The English government is prohibiting Egypt from exporting wool to Japan, and Canada is expected to announce that it will stop copper exports to Japan. [Note that this was more than a year before the Japanese attack on Pearl Harbor.]

No news of convoy traffic in the North Atlantic. Spanish sources have reported a grey-painted auxiliary cruiser near Cape Finisterre and one unidentified freighter heading north. A flotilla of patrol boats is heading south. There is also one heavily laden freighter with a one destroyer heading north. A group consisting of 10 light escorts, including one destroyer, and three freighters is heading east from Gibraltar. Two units are on the move from Freetown to England. These could be battleships. The cruiser *Caradoc* has been located off Canada and the cruiser *Cornwall* is near the French coast.

Air reconnaissance has reported nine convoys: 33 ships heading south and 56 ships heading north, between Dover and Great Yarmouth. Fourteen destroyers, three motor torpedo boats, 34 patrol boats and four minesweepers have been detected in the area around the Humber.

5 October

Reports from English aircraft have provided an insight into convoy movements some 125nm west of the Hebrides and northwest of the Orkney Islands. Portuguese sources have reported that a convoy has left Lisbon yesterday for England. An English warship, adrift near Sunderland after an explosion, is asking for assistance. A sinking ship has been identified off Hartlepool and a minesweeper is on its way to assist. Two cruisers are heading south near Jutland. Very little ship movements have been detected in the English Channel, but one motor torpedo boat has been reported to be north of Cherbourg (France).

6 October

An agent in Lisbon has reported the departure of a convoy consisting of 18 ships including five colliers with pit props for England. An English patrol boat has been sunk to the west of Cape Trafalgar. Six convoys consisting of about 122 freighters and over 10 escorts

are on the move through English coastal waters. There is heavy traffic in the Thames estuary. A number of patrol boats are known to be between Dover and Dungeness, but there appears to be no other traffic in the Channel.

7 October

Radio messages from English aircraft have provided an insight into convoy activities to the north of Ireland, in the North Channel and in the Irish Sea. Radio direction finders indicate much of this traffic is concentrated in the North Channel. Two naval ships, which had left Dakar, have appeared in the Irish Sea and are now probably in some shipyard for repairs or maintenance. *Renown* and four destroyers have arrived at Gibraltar. Some naval vessels, probably escorting a convoy or troop transports, have arrived either off Kenya or Aden.

An unidentified English authority has prohibited ships sailing in the areas Portland, Alderney, Cherbourg and The Needles (Isle of Wight). The reason for this is not clear.

8 October

Air reconnaissance has reported five troop transports with a destroyer escort northwest of Ireland. A transporter to the west of the Hebrides, with two cruisers and destroyers, is heading north. The British passenger liner *Oronsay* (20,000grt) has requested immediate help due to engine failure as a result of a bomb hit. Spanish reports tell of fishermen who have seen four-engine reconnaissance aircraft in the area 49° 50'N 10°–11°W on a daily basis. At times there are larger formations of combat aircraft. The fishermen were instructed by the aircraft to leave the area. Attention is drawn to the attached B-Dienst Report 1740, which gives details of the routes being used by shipping from the Bristol Channel area to the north of Ireland.

There were four heavy ships in Freetown, possibly cruisers plus two aircraft carriers, three destroyers, two submarines and a large number of freighters. The B-Dienst has discovered that the Commander-in-Chief of the 1st Cruiser Squadron, flying his flag on *Devonshire*, has moved from Scapa Flow to the Freetown–Nigeria area. The cruiser *Cornwall* has also been located in this area.

9 October

Radio messages from English aircraft have provided an insight into convoy procedures. An HX convoy heading 135° has been detected. According to Norwegian seamen aboard a Finnish ship there are no English mines in the Denmark Strait. It is assumed that *Renown* is in Gibraltar. *Barham* and *Resolution* were in Freetown and are now on their way to England. *Revenge* is in Canadian waters, the aircraft carrier

Hermes off Aden and *Ark Royal* and *Argus* off Freetown. Task Force M, including *Cornwall* and *Delhi*, is also off Freetown. For the location of other heavy ships see B-Dienst Report 1145.

Our intercept stations have picked up numerous messages addressed to the Commanding Officer for Minesweeping in the Thames estuary. These are probably reporting the sighting of the latest German mines which have been deposited in The Downs [off Deal].

British radio has announced that Dutch lifeboats are not sailing under the protection of the Red Cross and they are to be considered to be enemy ships. The crews are to be treated as traitors.

10 October
Intercepts from messages transmitted by British aircraft have, once again, given an insight into convoy activity to the west of Ireland and in the North Channel area. One battleship, the heavy cruiser *Cumberland*, three destroyers and five patrol boats have arrived in Gibraltar. The cruisers *Devonshire*, *Cornwall*, *Dorsetshire* and *Shropshire* are off Freetown.

11 October
Transmissions from English aircraft have provided information about convoy movements in the Irish Sea, the Liverpool area and in the North Channel. Patrol boats have been detected near Cape Finisterre.

Four transports with troops on board have separated from a convoy which left Gibraltar on 9 October. Further details are given on the enclosed sheets.

Radio intercept stations have established that the following ships are near Freetown: Commander-in-Chief of 1st Cruiser Squadron aboard *Cornwall*, *Delhi*, and the auxiliary cruiser *Asturias*. Further away, along the South American east coast, is Task Force M with Commander-in-Chief of the South American Division and the auxiliary cruisers *Alcantara* and *Queen of Bermuda*. These are expected to run into Rio.

There has been a lot of radio activity in the English Channel and along the English east coast. This was especially heavy at around midnight.

A summary of enemy activity has been provided on separate papers.

Above: The cruiser HMS *Devonshire* which fired the final torpedoes at the sinking *Bismarck*. She was to serve in both the Home Fleet and the Eastern Fleet during the war. *IAL*

12 October

The cruiser *Cumberland* at Gibraltar has turned out to be *Australia*, which has left last night together with battleship *Renown* and four destroyers, heading in a westerly direction. There have been a number of Operational Priority signals in the Gibraltar area from early morning until about 10.00 hours giving tactical type of information. English units, probably submarines, have been detected off Cape Finisterre and in the Bay of Biscay. Later there were indications of surface ship activity in the Finisterre area.

14 October

Convoy HX77 was near the southern exit of the North Channel and an outward-bound convoy further west off Northern Ireland. A battleship, probably *Renown*, and three destroyers have arrived in Gibraltar from the west.

The Commander-in-Chief of the 1st Cruiser Squadron is also Commander-in-Chief of Task Force M. A number of large ships have been reported as being visible from the Cameroon coast.

15 October

Radio direction finders have detected the presence of an unidentified English squadron to the west of Portugal. In addition to *Renown* and three destroyers, one cruiser of the *Birmingham* class arrived yesterday in Gibraltar, together with the battleship *Barham*, a heavy cruiser and three destroyers, which have all come from the west.

Two large eastbound convoys have been detected by the Radio Monitoring Service off Northern Ireland and the commotion in the airwaves was created by the dispersal of the merchant ships to various ports.

English aircraft in the Channel area have been instructed not to report the presence of their own ships off Dunkirk and not to harass any such activity. This task force, which was detected by the B-Dienst in good time, has bombarded Dunkirk from a considerable distance and was forced to break off its action by the battery *St Pol*. There is considerable minesweeping activity along England's southeast coast.

18 October

Battleship *Barham* is now in a recently completed dock in Gibraltar for repairs. It would appear as if the ship has a jagged hole about a metre in diameter just below the waterline.

19 October

The Admiralty has announced that Vice-Admiral John Tovey has replaced Admiral Sir Charles Forbes as Commander-in-Chief of the Home Fleet. Rear-Admiral Sir Henry Harwood [Squadron Commander in the South Atlantic during the Battle of the River Plate with pocket battleship *Admiral Graf Spee*] has been appointed Lord Commissioner of the Admiralty and Chief Adjutant of the Admiralty Staff. Tovey is 55 years old and took part in the Battle of Jutland during World War 1. He commanded *Rodney* from 1932 until 1934 and was then Assistant to the 3rd Sea Lord until he was made Commander-in-Chief of Destroyers in the Mediterranean.

Radio direction finders have located a British unit some 120nm west of southern Norway. A patrol boat has sunk near Harwich after an explosion. Submarines have been detected northwest of Terschelling (Holland), north of Cape de la Hague and in the approaches to Le Havre harbour.

The cruiser *Augusta* left Manila yesterday with Shanghai reservists on board.

20 October

Countless submarine warnings, information about torpedoed ships and details of ships being towed confirms that there is a lot of U-boat activity off Northern Ireland. The British freighter *Maryland* is being followed by a suspicious ship, according to a report from a tanker.

An important convoy, which was supposed to have left Liverpool during mid-September, called in at Freetown, and is presently on its way to Cape Town. A large naval squadron is supposed to be in the South Atlantic to protect these ships.

22 October

Aircraft are being deployed to search for shipwrecked survivors in the area to the west of the Hebrides and there are minesweeping activities in the approaches to Liverpool.

During the evening monitoring stations intercepted a call from the Commander-in-Chief of the Western Approaches to the freighter *Port Fairy*, which reads: 'Was the destroyer sunk? Please send any information about survivors from the enemy ship.' This signal is rather important because it could concern *Ship 21*, which is on her way home. This signal from the Commander-in-Chief of the Western Approaches could suggest *Ship 21* has been sunk or is in difficulties. Obviously the authorities have not yet had any news from the destroyer in question and the freighter *Port Fairy* must have sent an earlier report which has not been intercepted by our radio monitoring stations. It could well be that *Ship 21* has run into a convoy and has then been attacked by the destroyer which managed to shoot a torpedo before *Ship 21* was able to engage her weapons. [*Ship 21* was the ghost cruiser or auxiliary cruiser *Widder* under Korvkpt Hellmuth von Ruckteschell, which left the Elbe estuary via Bergen on 5 May 1940 and then returned to Brest in France on 31 October 1940.]

Radio direction finders have located English activities in the middle of the Dogger Bank. The area from Harwich to Orford Ness is being cleared of mines, during which there were two accidents. One patrol boat and a trawler seem to have sunk and ships are searching for survivors. There is destroyer activity in the Thames estuary.

23 October
We have no recent news about convoy deployment. One English unit has been detected to the northwest of Ireland and there are destroyers in Donegal Bay searching for survivors from a sunken ship. This operation is being supported by air reconnaissance. Minesweepers have been out twice during the night to clear the approaches to Liverpool. New routeing measures for transatlantic convoys have been detected and the details are listed on the enclosed sheets. Seven heavy ships are anchored in Scapa Flow. There is one aircraft carrier and four heavy cruisers plus about 30 ships. These are mainly freighters with a few destroyers. Aerial reconnaissance would suggest some of the convoy routes have been readjusted to run further north due to the heavy U-boat activity in the more southerly areas. A heavy ship has been detected by radio direction finders some 120nm east of Newcastle. There have been a large number of radio transmissions from the northern North Sea, but the reason for this has not yet been established. There could be a special operation, increased patrols or even training exercises.

25 October
Once again the Radio Monitoring Service has obtained an insight into convoy movements from radio transmissions made by English aircraft; and heavy ships of fleet have been detected in the same area by direction finders.

The cruiser *Australia* has been detected in western Biscay, probably on passage from Gibraltar to England. A few days ago two destroyers were reported as having landed about 70 German, Italian and French prisoners of war in Gibraltar. These have been transferred to another ship making for England. It is said they have come from a ship sunk in the North Atlantic, but it is not known who they are or which ship they have come from.

Convoys SLS53 and SL53 are due to leave Freetown and we can assume that *U65* has just arrived in that area. Two British Operational Priority signals have been intercepted from there.

28 October
Admiral Devonport has asked the British freighter *Mahout* to specify whether an earlier sighting report of a suspicious ship concerned a merchant ship or a warship. This, together with other signals, would suggest that the enemy is counting on there being another breakout of German merchant raiders.

The earlier report from the freighter *Port Fairy* of a destroyer and the possible sinking of a German ship has also been clarified. It would appear that this sinking was the result of a collision in the western Atlantic and *Port Fairy* is heading towards Bermuda with a number of survivors. At around the same time, the Admiralty has announced the sinking of the Canadian destroyer *Marguerite* (earlier *Diana*) as a result of a collision with a merchant ship.

The British freighter *Sandown Castle* has reported the presence of a suspicious ship.

29 October
The cruiser *Australia* and another large ship have been detected towards the west of Ireland and these are probably the suspicious ships mentioned yesterday by *Mahout*.

Cornwall is in the eastern section of the North Atlantic on her way to Plymouth; the auxiliary cruiser *Alcantara* in western Biscay and in radio communication with the Commander-in-Chief Western Approaches. Both these ships had been in African waters until recently. It is possible that they are escorting an important convoy or they are due to be replaced by others. It is possible that two ships are also on their way south, since this would correlate with reports from Spanish fishermen.

Radio monitors have discovered the course of the freighter *Larrinaga*, which left Baha Blanca yesterday and is due in Freetown on 14 November. The exact course details are on the enclosed sheet. As can be seen from these figures much of this route lies within the Pan American Neutrality Zone and shows quite clearly that the enemy is making use of this zone, which our raiders have been told to avoid.

A submarine has been detected off Norway and there has been very active English air reconnaissance over the North Sea. There is also considerable coastal convoy traffic along the east coast. Motor torpedo boats have been located near Grimsby and Lowestoft.

30 October
Radio direction finders have discovered a number of deep sea tugs trying to salvage ships north of Ireland. This would suggest they have been damaged by U-boats. The Commander-in-Chief for U-boats was immediately informed.

The *Empress of Japan* (26,000grt), coming up from the south, has received special instructions from the Admiralty and is to pass out of sight of the Cape Verde Islands. Similar instructions have been given to three other ships during the last few days.

An English freighter has reported having been hit by a torpedo near Aberdeen, but a mine seems a more likely cause.

Four freighters have run aground near Rattray Head and have asked for assistance. Tugs and rescue ships have been sent to the area. English air reconnaissance has reported a dispersed convoy of 12 ships, four escorts and one cruiser southeast of Kinnaird Head. The five dropped-out ships probably came from this convoy. A further ship has been reported to be drifting and to be unmanoeuvrable in the Moray Firth. This was stranded some time later to the southwest of Noss Head. It is possible that these ships were partly damaged by mines.

The men of the French cruiser *Jeanne d'Arc* have declared themselves to be on General de Gaulle's side.

31 October
Task Force M in the South Atlantic, known to be consisting of *Devonshire* and *Delhi*, has been joined by *Shropshire* and *Dorsetshire* in the Bay of Guinea. *Dragon* is probably in the same area.

English air reconnaissance has been active, searching the area from Scotland as far as Norway and Denmark. There is a strong conglomeration of merchant ships between Montrose and Noss Head. The usual minesweeping activities are taking place along the east coast. Little surface activity in the Channel, but there have been a number of air attacks against French coastal towns.

Below:
The British battleships *Warspite* (in the foreground) and *Resolution* (behind) were both of World War 1 vintage and served throughout World War 2. *IWM*

Index